Aloha Magnum

Aloha Magnum

Larry Manetti's
Magnum, P.I. Memories

LARRY MANETTI
with CHIP SILVERMAN

Foreword by Donald P. Bellisario,
creator of *Magnum, P.I.*, *Airwolf*,
Quantum Leap, and *JAG*

RENAISSANCE BOOKS
Los Angeles

To anyone who had anything to do with the *Magnum, P.I.* television series, including, but not limited to, Universal Studios, the creator, the producers, the directors, the writers, the cast, the crew, and the people of the great state of Hawaii. And most of all, to the loyalty and devotion of the millions of *Magnum, P.I.* fans throughout the world.

Copyright © 1999 by Larry Manetti and Chip Silverman

All rights reserved. Reproduction without permission in writing from the publisher is prohibited, except for brief passages in connection with a review. For permission, write: Renaissance Books, 5858 Wilshire Boulevard, Suite 200, Los Angeles, California 90036.

Library of Congress Cataloging-in-Publication Data

Manetti, Larry
    Aloha Magnum : Larry Manetti's Magnum, P.I. memories / Larry Manetti with Chip Silverman ; foreword by Donald P. Bellisario.
      p. cm.
    Includes index.
    ISBN 1-58063-052-9 (alk. paper)
    1. Manetti, Larry 2. Actors—United States—Biography.
3. Magnum, P.I. (Television program) I. Silverman, Chip.
II. Title.
PN2287.M27A3 1998
791.45'028'092—dc21   98-39327
   [B]   CIP

10 9 8 7 6 5 4 3 2 1
Design by Tanya Maiboroda

Manufactured in the United States of America
Distributed by St. Martin's Press
First Edition

"Larry's the only guy I know who looks good cooking in a tuxedo; he's also the tallest short guy I know."
—JOHN LARROQUETTE

"I was fortunate enough to be able to give Larry his first break. When the film was finished, I knew he would be special, not only as an actor but as a person."
—ROBERT WAGNER

"Larry Manetti knows more stars and their secrets than I could even begin to name; not bad for a man who was upstaged by a kangaroo."
—DON BELLISARIO, co-creator of *Magnum, P.I.*

"Frank and I adored spending time with the Manettis. My husband loved working with Larry and Tom Selleck on *Magnum, P.I.* and we've been close friends ever since. Larry gave Frank and I "Rocky," a talkative yellow nape Amazon parrot, in Hawaii as a going-away present! He's protective and very ornery—and we love him dearly. Rocky quickly learned some rather colorful language from my husband, along with parts of "My Way," and often climbed down from his perch, walked across the living room to join us in the den for hors d'oeuvres—a very sociable bird! You're having a very colorful life, Larry!"
—BARBARA SINATRA

"*Magnum, P.I.* was my favorite show—after *Mannix*, of course. This book is a warm, entertaining, exciting, inside look at the makings of a popular number one series set in Hawaii. A must read by any TV viewer."
—MIKE CONNORS ("Mannix")

"Although I did not appear in the series, which was *Magnum, P.I.*'s loss, Larry and Tom and I became great friends."
—TONY CURTIS

"This book was written on cocktail napkins!"
—DENNIS FARINA

"I'm told I had a great time."
—JEFF MACKAY, *Magnum P.I.*'s Mac Reynolds

"When Larry was in school, I was told he had a magnetic personality and a million dollar smile, and that he would never amount to much. Surprise, surprise!"
—Larry's father, MARIO MANETTI

"If, as *Reader's Digest* tells us, laughter is the best medicine, Larry should have an M.D. after his name. He has kept me in stitches with his quick remarks, funny stories, or typical Larry one-liners. His standard prescription would be 'keep on smiling and keep on laughing.'"
—FRED PILUSO, President, Scruples Beach Club

"*Magnum* was an era all by itself that has disappeared. Larry is still an era all by himself, thank God! We were all great friends, and that friendship and camaraderie showed on screen. That's what made the show a special experience for each of us."
—ALAN J. LEVI, director, *Magnum, P.I.*

Contents

$\mathcal{A}$cknowledgments

W e are greatly indebted to Renee Collins-Silverman for her immense contributions and patience in working on every facet of this book.

We also wish to acknowledge Brenda Scott Royce, our editor at Renaissance Books, for providing us with direction and advice.

Additionally, we are thankful to the following individuals for providing materials, memories, information, and assistance for the book: Nancy DeCarl, Don Bellisario, Peter Terranova, Fred Piluso, Tim Ryan, Bob Litwin, Charles Johnson, Scott Hart, and Ross Browne.

And, of course, special thanks to our agent, Frank Weimann.

Foreword

Long before *Magnum, P.I.*, I was a writer-producer on *Baa Baa Black Sheep* when Larry Manetti burst into my life with his Chicago accent and bantam rooster cockiness. "I'm Italian. You're Italian," he proclaimed. "Why are you cutting my scenes?!"

Telling Larry the truth—that the script was too long and his scene was extraneous—would have been like pouring Tabasco sauce on a hot Italian sausage. So, I lied—sort of. I said I knew a way to make him stand out from the rest of the ensemble. Naturally he wanted to know what it was. I smiled like a man with a secret (the secret was that I had no idea) and asked him to be patient and he'd read it in the next script.

For a moment it looked like Larry was going to give me the Sicilian kiss of death. Instead he invited me to his house for spaghetti and sausage. By the time I got there I knew what I was going to do. It made Larry a standout in the rest of the episodes and almost prevented him from ever having children.

As to what we did . . . it's in the book.

And despite all the complaining, Larry must have secretly liked it because twenty years later I'm still going to his house for spaghetti and sausage.

—Donald P. Bellisario
Creator and executive producer
of *Magnum, P. I.*

Chapter 1

Magnum, P.I.: The Beginning

A few years ago I was flying to Hawaii to do a new show called *Marker* for United Paramount Network. They had asked me to join the cast because they needed someone with energy. Looking out the window of the Hawaiian Air plane, I thought to myself, *Jesus, this must be at least the hundredth time that I've taken this trip.* I reclined the seat and dozed off. When I woke up, I was thinking about the time, back in 1980, I was playing tennis on the rooftop of one of the hotels in Honolulu with an actor-friend of mine by the name of W. K. Stratton. I was there to film the pilot for *Magnum, P.I.* As he served the ball, Stratton said, "Manetti, you're gonna be here for ten years."

"Like hell," I said. "This pilot's in and out. Nobody's gonna want to watch a bunch of coconuts."

It all started the day Don Bellisario phoned me to pitch his latest show. This was years before he became well known for creating *Quantum Leap.*

"I'm writing this great role for you," he said. "Custom-tailored to Larry Manetti. I'm gonna dress you in a white sport coat, surround you with beautiful women, and give you your own nightclub called Rick's Cafe Americain."

The stars of Magnum, P.I.—*me, Tom Selleck, Roger E. Mosley, and John Hillerman.*

"Sounds great, Don, but I'm up for another series, something called *Simon & Simon*. I don't know..."

A moment of silence followed. "Look, you don't even have to *act* in this," Bellisario said. "I mean, come on, let's face it, you're no Laurence Olivier."

"This is supposed to persuade me?"

"All I mean is, you just have to play yourself, add some pizzazz. The rest is a walk in the park."

I first met Don Bellisario when he began as a writer on *Baa Baa Black Sheep*. The show, which was renamed *Black Sheep Squadron*, lasted two seasons. It had a large cast of regulars, all consummate actors—including Robert Conrad, John Larroquette, and Simon Oakland. In the series, Conrad played Major "Pappy" Boyington, commander of a squadron of misfit flyers in the South Pacific. Pappy was a maverick who didn't care about discipline or regulations, and as a result his men got into plenty of mischief. I played one of the nonconformist fly-ers, Lieutenant Bob Boyle.

Conrad has done several movies and TV series, but he's probably best known for his hit 1960s series, *The Wild Wild West*. John Larroquette went on to star in *Night Court* as well as his own series, *The John Larroquette Show*. Simon Oakland was an older character actor who had costarred in *Night Stalker*, and was in the movies *Bullet* and *Tony Rome*, to name a couple.

During *Baa Baa Black Sheep*, I was still feeling my way around as an actor, trying not to bump into the furniture. I was mainly interested in whether my eyes looked real green and my hair was parted right. All of a sudden, fan mail started

The cast of Baa Baa Black Sheep *(left to right): Jeff MacKay, John Larroquette, me, Robert Conrad, Robert Ginty, Dirk Blocker, W. K. Stratton, and James Whitmore Jr.*

pouring in to the show, and I was getting a ton of it. I went from being a nobody to the top guy receiving all this fan mail. So NBC told the writers to start giving me more lines. Well, I wasn't really ready for this. I was having a hard time because, for me, memorizing lines was a very difficult task. People think acting is an easy job, but it's not. It's really tough.

Bellisario came on board as a new writer for *Baa Baa Black Sheep* about one year into the production. One day, I picked up a new script and saw that I'd gone from having these great scenes to getting only two lines. I freaked out and went flying into his office. I can still picture that moment with Don in his army shirt and glasses, smoking a cigarette. He looked up at me with these big blue eyes.

"Hey you, my name's Manetti!" I shouted.

"Sit down," he ordered.

"I'm pissed!" I screamed.

"Sit down!" he yelled louder.

"I worked real hard to get where I'm at. You got me doin' two lines!"

"So what's the matter with that?"

"I want to stand out in the show," I pleaded. "I want to be a star." I was really full of myself then.

"You do, huh?" he said with a grin. "I'll tell you what. Let me think about it. Next week, when I write the next script, I promise I'm gonna give you something in every episode that people will never forget. And neither will you."

I shook his hand. "Deal, pal."

The next week, the opening scene began with a cargo carrier in the South Pacific. The door opened and two drunken soldiers got off. Then I appeared, drunk, carrying a kangaroo named Rocky whose life dream was to kick me in the groin. Throughout the rest of the series, that was my pet, Rocky the kangaroo, who smelled to high heaven. I had to keep apples and feed him, too.

Don Bellisario was like a guardian angel to me, but he drove me crazy with the animals!

From that day on, I never messed around with Don Bellisario, although he still messed with me. A few episodes later, he added a myna bird to my role responsibility; but the myna bird and the kangaroo didn't get along very well. After the bird almost died, the veterinarian who visited the set said that we had to get rid of the bird.

In spite of Bellisario driving me nuts with the animals, I still had a lot of respect for him. He has had a pretty remarkable career in TV for a guy who started when he was around forty. Before that, he was a senior vice president and on the board of a large advertising agency in Texas. He had four kids, a wife, a big house, and a fancy car. But advertising was not his dream. He wanted to move on and try something different. It took him five years to convince his wife that television was his calling.

Don came from Pennsylvania, the product of an Italian father and a Russian mother. They were both fairly religious, so he grew up on a mixture of Russian Orthodoxy and Catholicism. Don used to talk about how he always celebrated two Easter and two Christmas holidays and how much he enjoyed it. He attended Penn State where he majored in journalism. In the middle of college he did a four-year hitch in the marines before going back to complete his degree. Bellisario was a newspaper journalist for a while and eventually ended up in the advertising world. It took him fifteen years to reach the big time.

After Don convinced his wife that he should work in television, he went out to Los Angeles, where he directed commercials and wrote screenplays. Eventually his agent introduced him to Stephen J. Cannell, a famous television producer who did *The Rockford Files* and *Baretta*. At the time, Cannell was the executive producer of *Baa Baa Black Sheep*. He gave Bellisario a chance at writing a script for him, and later hired him to be the story editor. After about a half dozen episodes, Cannell named Bellisario producer of *Baa Baa Black Sheep*.

Don told me that the *Magnum, P. I.* executives brought him on board because the star didn't like the way his character was originally written—too much of a macho man who always got the girls and never made a mistake. Bellisario rewrote and revised the character of Thomas Magnum and, in the process, changed the entire concept of the show.

It was also Bellisario's idea to give *Magnum*'s Hawaii a different look. He knew that TV viewers had been watching *Hawaii Five-O* for over ten years, and he wanted to use different locations. So he found a way to shoot most of the scenes on the windward side of the island. It had more of a pre-World War II Hawaii look that Bellisario wanted to project—the true paradise that Hawaii was forty years ago.

When he pitched *Magnum* to me I liked what I heard but wanted to know more, especially about the character he kept saying was just like me. I was real interested in Rick's obsession with Humphrey Bogart.

"You'll even have a piano player named Sam," Bellisario continued.

"Sounds good, I've got to admit. Who plays Magnum?"

"A new guy. I think you'll like him," he added. "His name's Tom Selleck."

"Tom *Selleck*? Sign me on!"

"I take it you've heard of him?"

I had. We worked together on a *Rockford Files* episode in 1979. Selleck played a detective named Lance White who always wore a white suit, always got the girls, and always solved the crime. It was no wonder he didn't light up over the original *Magnum* pilot. It was the same character.

I remember the first day of that *Rockford* shoot; I was sitting with Simon Oakland in a packed auditorium at 6:30 in the morning.

"Who's playing this Lance White guy?" I asked Simon.

"Someone I've never heard of. All I know is, he's supposed to look like Clark Gable."

There were maybe fifteen hundred people in the room, making quite a racket as they talked, drank their coffee, and ate their donuts. Then all of a sudden the room went so quiet it felt like my hearing had gone or something. I looked up and there was Tom Selleck, looking like some kind of knight in shining armor. He was decked out in all white—suit, shirt, tie, even his shoes.

"Jesus, Simon," I said, "he's prettier than any woman in here. And don't think I haven't checked them all out."

Now Selleck was walking through the room and the women were going nuts. Hell, so were the guys.

Tom and I got along great right from the start, and after the first day of shooting, we decided to get together for dinner. That night, there was a girl coming to see me from New York, a top model. When she arrived, she just stared at Tom. He took me aside and said, "Larry, I really like her." Then she took me aside and asked, "Larry, would you mind if I went out with him instead of you tonight?" Now, I'm no chopped-liver guy, so this was a big slap in the face. But I reluctantly told her, "No, I don't mind. Go ahead."

So when Don told me it was Tom Selleck for *Magnum, P.I.*, I thought, *I've got to be an idiot not to do this pilot. This could be it.*

With Tom Selleck playing Magnum, I knew we had the chance for a hit. But I also had reservations, and not just because any pilot is basically a crap shoot. Don Bellisario had done nine pilots before—every one a failure. But when he told me about Selleck and described my character, I figured, *Hawaii, a red Ferrari, an estate, two Doberman pinschers, a million girls in bikinis running around on the beach, and me—how could we miss?*

So I'm in Hawaii playing tennis and thinking about the role I'm supposed to play. That afternoon at four, we had to shoot the scene that appears in the opening credits of the early episodes of *Magnum*: me in a rickshaw wearing a straw hat kicked back over my eyes with the caption: "starring Larry Manetti." What I wasn't told was that before I could sit in the rickshaw, I had to peddle the thing with a passenger in the back of it. Bellisario was directing, and I was peddling my ass off. I delivered my dialogue and Bellisario said, "Cut! Okay, do it again." So I had someone drive the cart-like bicycle back to the start. We did over fifteen takes, and I almost went to the hospital suffering from exhaustion. That was my first day on the set of *Magnum*.

After filming the pilot, I returned to L.A. and waited to hear whether CBS and the affiliates were going to pick it up as a series. The longer we waited, the more pessimistic I became. So I went scouting around, looking for a movie or TV bit to do.

In those days, I was carefree. I didn't care about money. If I made $5,000 doing a show, I would spend $7,500. I was always trying to catch up, because I was either living in a penthouse that was too expensive, driving a convertible I couldn't make the payments on, or entertaining women I couldn't afford. I didn't care. I owed money to every restaurant in town, but I eventually paid them.

One day my agent, David Shapiro, was going nuts looking all over L.A. for me. It was around cocktail time when he finally reached me on the phone; I was in a bar with a bunch of people. He said, "You're not going to believe it! CBS showed the pilot to all the affiliates and they went nuts. You got a twenty-two episode order. You're going to Hawaii!"

A couple weeks later, CBS had all of the show's regulars appear at the Century Plaza Hotel for a meeting with the affiliates, the local TV stations from all over the United States. We were introduced on stage, and then we had to meet the station representatives. After half an hour, I said, "Screw it. This is boring. I'm leaving." Selleck grabbed me. I remember this because they were more worried about me than anyone else. Selleck, John Hillerman, and Roger Mosley were very cordial. Not that I wasn't, but I could be hyper.

"Don't start," whispered Selleck while we were on the stage. "You can't be flip, and don't be so cocky!"

"I'm tired," I said. "Let's go."

He said, "You can't do that. You gotta stay here." Thank God for Thomas!

CBS also threw a party for all the affiliates so they could mingle with the cast. They loved it. We were not asked, we were *told* by the network, "You'd better be there, you'd better behave, you'd better not get drunk, and you'd better not do this or that!"

Then it was on to pre-production and preparation. I went to wardrobe where they took my measurements. Most studios get stuff from places like J. C. Penney or they say, "You have to buy your own clothes." I told them that I had some things wrong with me—one arm was shorter than the other; I was born with a deformed leg—so, a tailor would have to custom-make all of my clothes. The guy in wardrobe believed me, and I'm not saying who he was. I wound up with all these beautiful tailor-made suits and shirts. Every stitch of clothing that was made for me in the nine years that we filmed, I kept. I still wear them.

I even had higher elevator shoes made because Tom was six-foot-four, and I would have looked foolish standing next to him. They made a dozen pair of these gorgeous shoes for me, which I also kept. Hell, who else was going to wear them?

Years ago, I was in a movie with Ed Asner and Stockard Channing called *The Girl Most Likely To....* In one scene I had to run up a hill, which was tough because I was always wearing elevator boots. I'm five-foot-seven, but, as usual, I was trying to look six feet tall. Anyhow, I couldn't run up this hill. It was too steep, and I slipped and started to roll backwards. Asner came up and stared at me. "Take those 'Manettis' off and put on some gym shoes," he ordered.

From that time on, everybody who worked with me in Hollywood referred to elevator shoes as "Manettis."

The fact that *Magnum, P.I.* would be shot entirely on location in Hawaii was not a plus for me. Not being a golfer or the beach-bum type, I knew there wouldn't be much for me there. I like Los Angeles, New York—big cities where there's plenty to do. As it turned out, the more I complained about Hawaii, the more the writers loved it and the more everybody thought I was perfect for the character of Rick.

Tom was laid-back, right at home on the beach. He loved to swim in the ocean. I was uptight about the ocean, terrified of sharks, and seldom swam further than the other end of a Jacuzzi. It was a contrast the writers thought served the story well. They also thought Tom Selleck was as perfectly matched to the location as he was to his role on the show.

All of the series' regulars were on *Magnum* from the beginning to the end, eight and a half years: Roger E. Mosley, John Hillerman, me, and Tom. Branscombe Richmond, who costars as the Indian bounty hunter on *Renegade* (another series created by Stephen J. Cannell), was the parking lot attendant at Rick's Cafe Americain in the original two-hour pilot. But aside from him, the original cast never changed.

Obviously, I was wrong about the *Magnum, P.I.* pilot being "in and out." I thought people wouldn't want to tune in each week to watch a bunch of coconuts, but they did tune in—for eight long years—to see Tom Selleck, the beautiful Hawaiian scenery, the red Ferrari, John, Roger, and last but not least, me.

Chapter 2

From Chicago to Hollywood

I attended St. Joseph's Military Academy and flunked second grade twice. After that, I went to St. Giles, a parochial school, where I fell in with a rough group of kids. My neighborhood, Oak Park, became a melting pot for many kids whose dads were, as we called it, in the Outfit or the Mob. These families had moved in soon after they made some money from their shady endeavors.

I started getting into trouble at St. Giles. Every year my behavior grew worse, and I never officially graduated from grammar school. They threw me and another kid out and mailed our diplomas to our homes. We didn't deserve the diplomas, but the school officials wanted to make sure that we never returned.

Junior high saw no improvement in my behavior or grades. The only thing I did that made my parents proud happened outside of school. When I was about twelve years old, I used to hang out at a gym in Chicago. I was there one day when they were filming scenes for the movie *The Golden Gloves Story*. The casting people needed a kid to fight in the ring, so they picked me. Even though I was pretty young at the time, it

Me at age eleven—a tough kid from a rough neighborhood.

made a lasting impression on me. It also kept my parents from disowning me.

My father decided to send me to St. Thomas Military Academy in Minnesota, one of the strictest and roughest boys' high schools. It was run by an ex-military officer named Colonel Calhain. He walked around with a cane, and it was rumored that he'd break it over your head if you did anything wrong.

The first day that I was there, I awoke to the sound of a bugle blaring in the hallway at six a.m. I thought, *What is this? Some idiot wakes you up at six o'clock in the morning blowing a bugle?* I watched where the bugle boy put his instrument, and later that day, I snatched it and threw it out the window. The bugle landed high up in a tree, and I slept peacefully the next morning. However, somebody snitched on me. I found out who it was, caught him, and gave him a beating. For that, Colonel Calhain made me stand in the corner for four hours. If I wasn't standing at attention, he'd come by and crack me with his cane.

Most of the kids at St. Thomas were scholars from well-to-do families; except for me and one other kid. We were constantly in trouble and were earning straight F's. There were study halls and help classes after school, but we never attended them. Instead, we climbed over the fence and walked for miles to find girls, returning only for dinner. At night, we would slip out the window again and look for the girls' schools. Inevitably, we were caught and punished, and threatened with expulsion. My father even offered to fund a new library to keep me there, but it didn't help. I was expelled after six months.

Returning to Chicago, I was placed in Oak Park and River Forest High School, where I didn't last long. The day I turned sixteen, I quit school altogether.

"Either you get a job or get out of the house," my father ordered. So I moved out of the house.

I decided that I would be a gangster. In my neighborhood, that was like a kid saying he was going to be a doctor or a dentist. It seemed easy. You dressed well and drove a nice car. Naturally, I didn't realize all of the other stuff that went with it. Since I'd grown up in an area where mobsters congregated, I figured I'd go right to the top to seek employment. One afternoon, I got up the nerve to approach the "boss of bosses"— Sam Giancana—in a restaurant. He was a golfer, and I used to see him on the driving ranges and golf courses, and later in restaurants and nightclubs that I frequented. I was drinking in bars with phony IDs when I was fourteen.

"So you want to learn the rackets, huh?" he asked.

"Yeah," I said, "that would be neat."

He grabbed my hand and pretended to put a pistol in it. "If I put a gun in your hand," he asked, "do you think you could use it?"

I went white when he said that because I knew what he meant. It wasn't like putting a rifle in your hand and going off to war. It was putting a handgun in your palm and going off to pop somebody.

"No," I answered, "I know I can't do it."

"That's good," Giancana said, smiling, "because a lot of guys say that they can and they wind up dead in a trunk."

When I was hanging out in the nightclubs in Chicago as a teenager with fake credentials, I met a comedian named Joey Villa. He was a few years older than me, but we developed an instant rapport. Sometime later, I took my first trip to New York with Joey, who was going to open for Bobby Darin at the Copacabana.

Back in those days, pretty rough hoods hung out at the Copa. When Joey and I went into the club one afternoon, I pointed out to him how tough certain guys were. I explained to him who this guy was and who that guy was, and so forth. While I was doing this, Joey bumped into a notorious gangster. The gangster grabbed him, shoved him into the wall, and asked, "Who are ya?"

"I'm the comedian," said Joey, sweating bullets.

"Are ya funny?" he asked.

"No," answered Joey. He was scared out of his wits.

After the show that night, the hood approached Joey. He threw his enormous arm around him, shook his hand, and smiled.

"I like you, kid," he said. "You're a man of your word."

〜〜〜

My father owned a plastic manufacturing company. He supplied probably 90 percent of the electronics industry with all kinds of components for televisions: tubes, sockets, and many other items. This was before the Japanese became the primary manufacturers of television equipment and parts. My father also manufactured ceramic and plastic wall tile, which was a big business years ago. Later he owned Tampa Downs, a development company in Tampa, Florida that sold homes. He was a very successful businessman.

My dad figured if I wasn't going to school, I'd better start working, so he got me jobs working on the docks and driving trucks for him. After doing this for a while, I came to realize that I had made a mistake. I'd look around and see guys much older than me with families, and I didn't know how they made it. They were really struggling.

I decided to try my hand at sales. I sold Britannica Encyclopedias, hustling them door-to-door. My sex life became quite active with the older women (over twenty-five then) who were home alone during the day. I'd stop by to sell them encyclopedias, and the next thing I knew I was in bed with them. Of course, I didn't sell very many encyclopedias.

Most of the ladies I met had sad tales to tell. They drank heavily and told me how every night their husbands would come home and beat them for no reason at all. My eyes were opened to the problems of abused women, long before it became public in the 1980s.

Later, my dad got me a job in the construction business. I remember standing on a scaffold, halfway up the side of a building, on a windy, blustery, winter day in Chicago, thinking, *There's got to be more to life than this.*

I made a deal with my father. "Listen," I said, "I want to go back to school, but I want to finish quickly. I don't want to screw around."

I hated Oak Park High and had a hard time learning there. I think I was hyperactive or had ADD, attention deficit disorder. Surely, had Ritalin been available in the 1950s and 1960s, I would have been an excellent candidate for the drug. But at that time, I just couldn't comprehend. As an actor, I have more memorizing and homework to do than I ever had in school, but I'm much more focused now. Back then, it was tough to keep my attention on anything long enough for it to sink in.

I went to the Central YMCA in downtown Chicago to earn my high school equivalency diploma, attending day, night, and Saturday classes. I wasn't working during that time because my father said that if I received good grades I didn't have to. I took every course I could and wound up graduating seven months before my high school class. It was a great feeling for me and my father, because we realized that I could actually accomplish something. He had really thought I was a lost soul.

After I received my high school diploma, I went back to work for a couple of my father's companies doing odd jobs. I was on a roof one day standing on a piece of plywood. A strong gust of wind suddenly blew the plywood upward like a parasol. I only weighed 130 pounds. I flew off the roof, into the air, and almost got killed.

I quit that job and went to work for a plumber. The first day at work, I was fifteen feet below the ground in mud and stench when I heard a whistle.

"What was that?" I asked.

"They called lunch," said the plumber.

"Oh, good," I said. "How do you get out of here?"

"Don't worry," he said, "I'll bring your lunch to you."

"You mean I eat while I'm sitting in this crap?"

"Yeah," he answered, and he dropped down a bucket attached to a rope. There was a sandwich and some chocolate milk inside. That was my last day.

Then, my friend, Frankie, got me a clerk job selling mutual tickets at Sportsmen Park Racetrack. One day, a power failure at the track darkened the building, and out of nowhere, I felt a cold piece of steel underneath my chin.

"Give me all your cash! Don't make a sound or I'm going to blow the top of your head off."

I gave the robber all of the money. The power returned as I yelled, "Robbery, robbery, robbery!"

The track officials were not thrilled, and I'm sure they thought I stole the money. But two other clerks were also robbed, so the officials decided to take my word for it.

About a month later, I saw a beautiful girl rushing past. Without thinking, I jumped over the counter and chased her, hoping to get her phone number. I left my open tray of money in plain view, and somebody leaned over and helped himself. When I came back, the money was gone, but I had the girl's phone number. They fired me.

That fall, I matriculated at St. Leo's, a brand new college in Tampa. It was the only place that would accept me. It was run by Catholic priests, and the student body was mainly comprised of misfits from all over the country. I soon realized that we all had one thing in common: none of us wanted to learn, we just wanted to screw around.

My father had a 1954 Buick convertible that he kept on a ranch he owned outside of Tampa. I forged his signature on a letter to the ranch foreman instructing him to give me the car. I wrote that I needed to drive here and there with my asthmatic aunt who had moved to the area. With the car, I was off to Miami, hitting every nightclub in southeastern Florida.

In order to finance my fun, I called my dad for additional money, telling him the system at the college had changed and that uniforms were now mandatory. He sent me a check for $1,200 to cover the cost. Then I told him that I needed money for food because I had developed an allergy to the college cuisine.

When the first semester grades were about to be mailed home, I broke into the Registrar's Office and changed my grades from F's and D's to A's and B's.

"I'm so proud," my dad said over the phone. "You're doing great!"

The next call he received was from the dean of students expelling me for failing. The ranch foreman helped me pack and drove me to the airport. I had lasted less than a year.

Upon my return to Chicago, I attended Loyola University for about six months, but I had a really hard time retaining information, so I dropped out.

Again, I went to work for my father, this time as a salesman of the ceramic tile and bathroom goods that he manufactured and distributed. I had a territory, and drove around making cold calls. Not only did I hate selling, but I was extremely unsuccessful at it. Dad knew this because during the sales meetings where we were pumped up with the motivating incentive of trips and gifts, he'd see the graphs and charts denoting sales by lines on a scale. Mine didn't even have a dot. I didn't sell anything.

But Dad was good to me. I received a paycheck, regardless, and I'd use the money to run around and go out with girls. Actually, I went to work every day to rest because I was out all night. Turning off the lights and locking the door to my office, I'd put my feet up on the desk and go to sleep.

Twice a week, I'd leave the office early to attend drama courses at Northwestern University. As a result, I was selected for roles in small theater productions of *Come Blow Your Horn*, *The Heiress*, and *Barefoot in the Park*. Robert Urich and John Reilly, who became a soap opera star, were also in these shows.

Robert Urich (*Vega$* and *Spenser: For Hire*) and I first met well over twenty-five years ago, when he was in Chicago trying to become an actor. He attended an acting class called the Ted Liss Acting Workshop while I was running around town like a wild man with my flashy girlfriends. One of the girls I was dating was Barbara Rucker. I introduced her to Urich, who is another Selleck, a great big, good-looking guy. After meeting him, she was no longer my girlfriend. Urich took off for Hollywood with her and they eventually got married. Bob became a close friend of Selleck's, too, and often visited him in Hawaii.

A girlfriend introduced me to an agent who got me a bit part in a United Airlines commercial. There was no speaking role for me and all I did was sit there. At that moment, I realized if I wanted to get any further, I needed to learn everything there was about acting. Through another girlfriend, I was fortunate enough to find a great acting coach in Chicago. One of the things the coach told me was that I needed to learn to speak without my Chicago accent.

Eventually, I quit my sales job, and, with a buddy of mine named Billy Kent, opened two joints in Chicago—Cockney Pride and the Faces Nightclub. Things were going great for me at the time. I was dating one of Chicago's top models, and I figured that the restaurant business was going to be very lucrative for me. But the restaurants didn't make it, and the girlfriends all wanted to get married. Marriage was like high school, I needed to drop out of that institution as well. So in September of 1972, I decided to take off for California.

I moved to L.A. because I felt that was the only way I would be discovered as a movie or TV actor. I drove my 1972 Jaguar cross county, not stopping until I reached Texas. I pulled into a gas station to ask for directions, but when I pulled out, I turned the wrong way following a pretty blond in a pickup truck. After a while, I drove through a neighborhood that I knew I'd passed before because it smelled terrible—it was around a slaughterhouse. I had driven the wrong way, halfway back across Texas. I turned around and headed back in the right direction, hoping this wasn't a sign of how things were going to work out for me in Hollywood.

Robert Conrad let me stay at his apartment when I arrived in L.A. I first met Conrad, whose career began as a singer, in 1968 in Chicago, through a mutual friend by the name of Imo Monoco. Imo was one of my father's business partners.

So here I was in L.A.—great car, great pad, no money, no friends. Hello, Hollywood! Hoping to meet beautiful women, I bribed a guard at Universal Studios to let me hang out at the commissary.

The only way I survived in Hollywood between loafing in the commissaries, meeting with agents, and trying to get into

TV and movies was by working odd jobs: construction, car sales, and bartending.

I drove cars to Mexico and sold them, and, on weekend nights, I tended bar at a place called the Butcher Shop in San Diego. Roberto, the owner, employed some of the most gorgeous girls in Southern California. It was *the* place to be. I was paid a decent salary and all the pizza and steak I could eat. I think that's where I developed an elevated cholesterol level.

One night I went to Tijuana with a buddy named Tug Marino who was visiting from Chicago. We hit all the nightspots before finally crashing in a two-bedroom suite at a hotel on the ground-floor level. In the middle of the night, I woke to movement in the room. I saw the shadowy figure of a man walk past my bed and into the other room. As I peered into Tug's room, the guy began to undress. He was kind of wobbly as he climbed into bed with Tug.

"Hey, Tug, watch it!" I yelled out.

Tug sat up and saw this naked guy crawling into bed with him. He picked up a lamp and cracked it across his head, putting the guy out cold.

When the police arrived, they found the guy dead. Instead of being congratulated for killing a burglar, the cops informed us that the dead guy was an officer of the Mexican Army, a federale, and arrested us.

The deceased had been very inebriated and attempted to sneak into his suite without his wife knowing. He thought he was crawling into bed with his spouse. We spent three days in a Mexican jail until the situation was resolved, then high-tailed it out of town. I've never been back to Mexico.

〰〰

One afternoon, I was sitting at one of the lunch tables in the commissary at Universal Studios with Robert Conrad, when Jack Webb came in. He told Conrad he was upset that he had to keep recasting his series, *Chase*. Jack turned to me and asked if I was an actor. I lied and said yes. He asked if I wanted a role, and I signed a contract immediately. The series didn't last for more than a few months, but it was the beginning of my acting career. I played a young detective.

At the beginning of my first episode, I was given my cue. "When the red light goes off," Webb, who was directing the episode, explained, "you jump out, point your gun at the crooks, and yell, 'Freeze!'"

However, hiding inside of this trash can, I could barely see the little red light. In addition, I hadn't been told which way to look after I jumped out. So when I jumped out the first time and yelled, "Freeze!" I was speaking to a telephone pole, and the bad guys were behind me. The second time, the same thing happened. On the third take, I really concentrated. But by the time I yelled, "Freeze!" the guys were running down the street, and I had to scream out again, "Freeze!"

"Listen, kid," said Webb, "even a perfectionist like Brando doesn't require three takes to say 'Freeze.' Get it right the next time or your career as an actor is history." I finally got it right.

A few weeks after I began doing *Chase*, Conrad invited me to Florida to act in a feature-length movie he was directing called *The Duke's Back in Town*. Even though I had only done some brief TV work, I convinced Conrad that I was an accomplished actor. I arrived on the set and they began shooting a few scenes.

After a few takes, Conrad called me over and said, "Larry, get serious. This is costing thousands of dollars."

"Whaddaya mean?" I asked.

"You're screwing around, aren't you? C'mon, start acting! I've got deadlines!" answered Conrad.

"But Bob, I am acting!"

They began filming again. After an hour, Conrad yelled, "Break!" He beckoned me over. "Listen kid, you're terrible. Go

With my great friend and mentor, Robert Conrad.

back to L.A. and get into acting school. You've cost me over a hundred grand today."

I was devastated, and I was disappointed in Robert Conrad—my mentor, my friend—not to mention that I was sick that everyone there thought I couldn't act. The cast and crew were all staring at me solemnly. No one said a word.

I was walking off the beach with my head down when Conrad called out to me. I turned around and saw the Duke (Conrad's nickname) standing by the camera. Everyone was laughing as the camera was opened. It was empty the whole time. The movie was never made.

Today, Conrad says he wasn't joking, he really thought I couldn't act.

〜〜〜

In 1973, Conrad and I opened a ski resort, the Last Run Saloon, in Bear Valley, California. It was a dream of his. He put up most of the money, and I put up Billy Kent who owned the two joints with me in Chicago. Kent became the general contractor and manager. It was a very rustic place with seventy-five rooms and lodges, and a fully staffed kitchen and bar. It was a huge investment.

On our opening night, we sponsored a pro-am celebrity race, which included Lloyd Bridges, Beau Bridges, Liza Minnelli, Clint Eastwood, and Mike Connors—a real star-studded event. After that, the place did pretty well for a while. Then, like all hotels and restaurants if they're not managed correctly, it went down the drain. I think it was one of the biggest disappointments in my life, and certainly one of Conrad's, because he really adored that place. It stayed open for about a year and a half. We had one guard there who would come in, drink, and fall off his seat, landing face down on the floor. His gun would slide down the bar. He was the entire security force.

One time, a bunch of us got into the Jacuzzi out back at around two-thirty in the morning. I accidentally pressed a button on the door and locked us out of the resort. There was no way to be rescued, so we had to break a window in the building. We built a huge snow bank, and Conrad had to stand on this seven-foot mountain of snow and push me through the broken window. Then I had to run through the hotel naked, awaken the night manager, and get a key. You can imagine what he was thinking when he woke up and saw me. After that, I ran back through the hotel lobby, shocking some late-night frolickers, but everyone was saved.

Another time, Conrad and I went to Las Vegas. We ran into a buddy of mine at the Stardust Hotel, and he gave me a new watch called a Pulsar. It had a black face, and when you pushed a button, red digits showing the time danced across the face. It was brand new at that time, and I really prized it.

That evening we went to see Elvis Presley perform, and Elvis introduced Robert Conrad during his act. After the show, we went backstage to see Elvis. We all shook hands. Elvis sat down next to me and started staring at my watch, mesmerized. Today, this type of watch is common, but back then it wasn't. I kept pushing the button to light it up, and Elvis went nuts.

Elvis took off a diamond ring he had on his pinky finger and said, "I'll trade you."

The diamond ring had to be worth a hundred grand. But I wouldn't part with my watch, and he got somewhat pissed off. The King was at the stage when he was just starting to deteriorate, although he still looked good. A couple minutes later, he introduced me to a former beauty queen.

He asked me again for the watch and said, "She's yours."

Again, I said, "No, thanks." Now Elvis began to sulk and wouldn't speak to me for the rest of the night.

The next day Conrad received a call from Red West, Elvis's bodyguard, who later became one of the regulars on *Baa Baa Black Sheep.*

"Elvis thinks your friend is a smart-ass son of a bitch," he said.

So the King wasn't real nuts about me, but that's because I wouldn't give him the watch.

∽∽∽

One of the places I wanted to visit during my first year in Hollywood was the Warner Bros. Studio because that was where they made all the old movies. I had my friend, Johnny Valentino, who lived in Los Angeles, drive me to the Warner Bros. lot.

"Geez," I said, "I'd really like to get inside."

"You can't," said Johnny. "They have guards."

I didn't care. I climbed a tree and lowered myself down over the fence, dropping onto the premises. Robert Forster's series, *Banyon,* was being shot, and I stared, mesmerized. A guard grabbed me. "All right, come with me," he ordered.

As the guard dragged me past the set, it caused a commotion, and Robert Forster glanced over at us.

"What's going on?" he inquired.

"I caught this kid," answered the guard. "He snuck in."

"Well," Forster said, "don't throw him out. Are you an actor, kid?"

"Yeah," I lied.

Lee Stalmaster was there and told the guard, "Let him go. He'll stand with me and watch the shooting." That's how I met her. She was one of the biggest casting directors in town. She asked me if I wanted a job, and I ended up working in her office part-time answering the phones and filing. Later, she got me a role in *Two Minute Warning*.

I had only a couple of lines in *Two Minute Warning*, but I received a lot of exposure. They had me in scenes hanging around behind John Cassavetes for three months, running up and down steps through a stadium. Finally, my big opportunity arrived on the last day of shooting. Larry Peerce, the director, had to leave for Aspen, Colorado, and he was in a real hurry. My lines were in the very last scene of the movie.

In this scene, another actor and I, playing SWAT cops, were sixty feet in the air in a light standard, which is a big lighting pole at the stadium. We were sitting up there, strapped in, holding rifles with scopes, looking for the bad guy. Director Peerce was standing in a bucket on a crane with the camera set up in front of him.

The director only gave us one take and one shot at this. "All right, my boy," he yelled at me in his booming voice, "get ready! On action, pick up the gun, aim, and fire. Then look at your partner, and say, 'I think I got him.' At that moment, you realize that your partner has been struck with a bullet and is dead. I want the reaction on your face to reflect that you've just lost your best friend."

The actor playing the other cop had never acted before. The makeup people had placed a blood pack—a small packet with an explosive—on his head. When a button was pressed, an electric shock hit the packet, which burst, making a popping sound as the blood squirted out. This inexperienced actor had no idea that this was going to occur.

Peerce screamed from the crane, "Are you guys ready?"

"We're ready," I yelled back.

He screamed, "Action!"

I heard a pop and blood gushed out on this guy's face.

"Goddamn it!" the actor yelled. "What the hell was that?"

"That's it!" Peerce exploded. "Cut!"

"What about my part," I pleaded, "my lines?"

"Sorry," Peerce replied, "I have to go to Aspen now. See ya later."

Here was my biggest break in a movie and that pseudo-actor blew it. I still remember how badly I wanted to kill him.

Right around the time that I was filming *Two Minute Warning*, Robert Conrad called and asked me to read for a part in the pilot of *Baa Baa Black Sheep*. I was sure I'd get the role. The only problem was that I was working on *Two Minute Warning*, so it looked like another one of those missed opportunities. Fortunately for me, the actor who was signed to play Boyle in the pilot dropped out before the show began filming. By then, I was finished with *Two Minute Warning*, and the producers asked me to read again.

I'll never forget when I learned I had the role of Boyle in *Baa Baa Black Sheep*. I called my dad back home in Chicago to tell him the good news, and, somehow or another, he misunderstood the message. He called back and consoled me on my answering machine, saying that he understood that I was the black sheep of the family, but that I was a lot better off than I used to be. Eventually, the message was unscrambled, but my dad was probably right.

When the show became a series, the character I was playing, Boyle, a real wisecracker like me, was generating so much fan mail that my role was expanded. Suddenly, I had a lot more lines.

It was 1974, my first year on *Baa Baa Black Sheep*, and I was on the way to judge the Miss Magic Mountain Beauty Contest. Stopping off at Von's Supermarket to buy ten Snickers bars (I didn't care about eating healthy back then), I spotted a gorgeous young woman and tried to pick her up. She put me off, advising me that she was a contestant in the Miss Magic Mountain contest, but might meet me later. I tried to fix the contest in hopes of having better luck with the pretty girl from the supermarket. It didn't work. The sponsor's girlfriend won. I think he must have been a better fixer than I was. My choice finished second and we began to date. Her name was Michelle Pfieffer.

I tried to help Michelle launch an acting career. She was just starting out and had no money. I introduced her to Jay Bernstein, a "star maker" who was responsible for the careers of Suzanne Somers and Farrah Fawcett among others. I told him he should take a chance on Michelle, she was going to be a big star. After meeting her, Jay called me up and said, "You're right, she's got a great face. But I can't take a chance because I don't know if she can act." I guess he lost out.

I took Michelle to Universal Studios with me one day. We saw Peter Terranova, who was then vice president of the studio. I knew Peter would tell Michelle if she had what it takes.

"Michelle," I said, as I pulled my car to a stop in front of Terranova, "show him your ass." Slowly she exited my car and turned around for his inspection. He nodded his approval and said, "You're going to hit the top." The rest is history.

〰

The cast of *Baa Baa Black Sheep* was selected to be in the Rose Bowl Parade. For some reason, Conrad wasn't available. They put the rest of us on a float, including John Larroquette, Simon Oakland, and me. It was a big mistake for the Rose

Bowl Parade Committee, which was chaired by Robert Wagner.

We were out of control, winging pies into the audience, splattering people. The pit bull used on *Baa Baa Black Sheep* was on the float with us. He was trying to bite us, so we kept throwing him off the float. After running and jumping back on every time, he managed to bite one of us. When the parade began, there were eight or nine of us on the float, and before the parade ended, it was empty. Everyone had jumped off to look for drinks.

The procession ended at the Magic Castle, where there was a buffet for all the participants in the parade. We started a food fight. As the manager walked into the room, we hit him with four pies.

Robert Wagner was livid and he called Conrad. The next day, Conrad lined us all up and was ready to fire us.

"All right, someone tell me what happened," he ordered.

I relayed the story about how we suckered the manager, who was a pompous sort of guy, into walking into the buffet before blasting him with the pies. Conrad broke up laughing.

"I know Wagner's pissed off," he said, "but this is one of the funniest stories I've ever heard."

Baa Baa Black Sheep was nominated for an Emmy at the same time *Roots* was up for all kinds of awards. That year, the Emmy people wanted everyone to come dressed in the outfits they wore in the various television shows. So our cast dressed in the period fashion of World War II in the Pacific.

We were sitting in the fourth row, pretty close to the stage. At one point, when they were announcing the Best Dramatic Series, *Roots*, we stood up and loudly applauded. All of a sudden I felt a huge hand grab me and sit me back down. Someone yelled, "Sit down! Don't you dishonor that uniform!"

I spun around with my fists ready. It was John Wayne, who was sitting directly behind me.

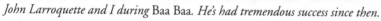

John Larroquette and I during Baa Baa. *He's had tremendous success since then.*

"Put those shoulders back," he ordered, "head erect, chest out, stomach in! You wear that uniform with pride, lad!"

I was aghast. I sat down, fairly shaken. Later that evening, after the show, we were backstage when I noticed a lot of people congregating around somebody. It was William Holden. I was so crazed at that point, I thought it was John Wayne. So when I got up in front of William Holden, I shook his hand and apologized for my posture, standing erect and saluting him. He looked at me as if I was some schmuck from outer space.

I met Peter Frampton in an L.A. bar, but was oblivious to who he was. He told me he was an English singer, and later, my future wife, Nancy, explained how famous he was. We were having an interesting conversation, and he said he really loved *Baa Baa Black Sheep.* I told the producers and Don Bellisario, who then wrote a great episode about Frampton being an

Australian who used to watch for enemy Japanese planes. In this segment, I was lost on an island, and the show revolved around Peter Frampton, me, and John Larroquette.

Black Sheep was the starting point for me, a learning period. The guys on the show were consummate actors, mostly trained in the theater. John Larroquette was one of them. We became instant friends and had a lot of fun together. At about six-foot-seven, he towered over me. John came from New Orleans where he had been a disc jockey. Like many young guys, he had his problems. Alcohol was one of them, and that is a known fact. Recovery is what his TV show, *The John Larroquette Show*, was all about. At that time, however, I really didn't know that any of the guys were problem drinkers. To me, they were just having a good time.

The cast of *Baa Baa Black Sheep* was large and it was decided for financial reasons that cuts had to be made. John Larroquette was let go. After that, John was pretty down-and-out for a while.

I remember seeing Larroquette months later at a read-through for a play called *The Last Mile*. I'll never forget it because it upset me terribly. John was messed up, really out of it. Then he somehow pulled himself together, and the next thing I knew he was costarring on *Night Court* and winning a whole bunch of Emmys. He had stopped drinking and straightened out his life. Now he has a great life, a happy family, and he's at the top of his career. I have tremendous respect for John Larroquette. When someone thinks he can't beat alcohol or drugs, he should think about John.

After *Black Sheep* was canceled, I was cast as a semi-regular on the futuristic ABC series, *Battlestar Galactica*. Following that, I got a role opposite Robert Conrad in another fairly short-lived series entitled *The Duke*.

In the early 1970s, the entertainment industry people with whom I dealt were still genuinely nice. In those days, they

*Conrad and I
(with Patricia
Conwell) starred
in another series,*
The Duke, *in
1979.*

would take a chance on you. Alan Goldstein was my agent, and he really believed in me. He took me around every day and helped me get my foot in the studios' front doors. Through him, I got roles in *Barnaby Jones, Cannon, Emergency, The FBI, Mannix, The Streets of San Francisco, Gunsmoke,* and *Switch,* among others.

It was during this time, working with some very professional actors, that I really learned a lot, much more than in drama school. I would say that the bulk of what I learned was from watching the actors on the sets of these TV shows.

I worked with the great actor Barry Sullivan (*The Bad and the Beautiful, Tell Them Willie Boy Is Here*) once. Later, I ran into him at a nearby bar.

"So, tell me," I asked as I approached him, "do you ever get to the point where you get bored being an actor?"

Sullivan turned around on his barstool and slapped me across the face.

"You never ask a question like that," he said. "Never ask an actor if he gets bored. We're artists."

I was so stunned that I didn't know whether to punch him out or buy him a drink.

I first met Patrick Duffy on the TV series, *Switch*, which starred Robert Wagner and Eddie Albert. Robert Wagner gave me probably my first big break as a guest star at the request of Bob Conrad. Patrick Duffy and I played police bomb experts in the episode. On the first day of filming, I was a nervous wreck. Only an actor knows this feeling: shaky knees, dry mouth, scared to death. It's you and you alone on camera, and nobody can help you. There's a crew of thirty or forty people behind this big eye that's staring at you with these glaring lights. I had a two-page scene where I had to explain how a bomb was made and how to defuse it. My speech contained some technical terms, real hard stuff to spit out, especially at that point in my career. Actors have a tendency, when they're young and new, to try to get all of their lines out as quickly as possible at the cost of not making any sense. So on the initial take, I rambled on and on.

Eddie Albert, who was playing opposite me, stopped me in the middle of my delivery with an ad lib.

"So listen, detective. Let's back up. Start from the beginning and tell me again. What's a spot bomb made out of and how do you defuse it?"

I just about dropped dead. We have a saying in the business about when you "go up." To go up means to forget your lines. I became nervous and intimidated, and I imagined that everyone was staring at me. After that, it was all uphill. I couldn't remember the first word, let alone a sentence. It was around take seventeen when I saw my career flying out of the window. I'll never forget how mad I was at Eddie Albert for throwing me like that, in the middle of a scene. I am not a big fan of his.

To the contrary, you couldn't find a better guy than Robert Wagner. If you don't like him, you don't like people. He's a class act.

I had a date with Connie Stevens in 1975, when she was at the top of her acting career. We went out to dinner, and, being extremely nervous in her company, I fortified myself with alcoholic beverages all night. Connie liked me and invited me back to her house in Bel Air, a 30,000-square-foot mansion.

By now, I was so intoxicated that I could barely navigate the entrance to the living room. Still nervous, I accepted her drink offer as I settled into a soft, cozy sofa. Connie disappeared to change into something more comfortable. Upon her return, I was asleep, snoring loudly.

She woke me up and threw me out of the house. It was, however, the beginning of a wonderful relationship.

My agent sent me to audition for a two-hour *Mannix* movie. I was waiting in the studio's greenroom for the initial interview. Seated next to me was another actor.

"Hi," I said, "my name's Larry Manetti."

"I'm Henry Winkler," he said.

"What are you here for?" I inquired.

"Oh, there's a pilot called *Happy Days*, and they want me to play this funky guy who walks around with greasy hair and a motorcycle jacket."

"I'm here for *Mannix*. I'm supposed to play a lawyer in a two-hour movie."

"Oh, wow," exclaimed Winkler, "I'd kill for that—working with Mike Connors."

"Well," I said, "if I meet him, I'll ask Mike if there's anything in the movie for you."

I wasn't able to help Henry Winkler with a job on *Mannix*, so he became the Fonz. Tough break!

I was playing the son of a Mafia chieftain on a *Streets of San Francisco* episode where I was killed and placed in a coffin. In the plot, no one was supposed to know that I was dead. I was placed in a secret compartment inside of the coffin, and another corpse rested over me.

"We're having trouble with the lights," the director said. "Let's break." The guy playing the corpse on top of me jumped out of the coffin, and as he did, he closed the top. I didn't hear the director, so I stayed put. Then I heard Michael Douglas telling someone that he'd be back later. I began to wonder how long I'd have to stay in the coffin.

Suddenly, I heard a guy announce, "Lunch!" I started yelling and kicking, but no one responded. Everyone had left, and I couldn't get out. I was screaming through this tiny breathing hole in the coffin, "Help! Help!"

After about twenty minutes, someone asked, "Who the hell is that?" It was Michael Douglas. He let me out of the coffin and handed me a glass of water. I was hyperventilating. He asked if I was all right.

"Yeah," I sighed, "but my acting career almost ended with me being buried alive."

On another *Streets of San Francisco* segment, I was playing a bad guy along with Robert Reed, who is best known as the father on *The Brady Bunch*.

The director explained the scene, "You run out of this place you just robbed, jump in a car, and squeal away. The tires burn and smoke. When I yell 'cut,' just slam on the brakes. That means you're out of range and the camera won't see you anymore."

I was very "green" then, and I didn't quite understand what was going on. The scene began and I hit the gas, the wheels spinning madly. The car flew like a jet. I was waiting for the director to say "cut," but the two-way radio wasn't functioning. Jimmy Luisi, who was playing a crook in the car with me, was doing a white-knuckle job on the dashboard.

"What are you doing?" he cried. "Slow down! Slow down!"

But I thought I was supposed to go through with the stunt. I saw a lot with a wooden fence and went for it. I hit the curb and the car sailed into the air, breaking through the fence and spinning around on the grass. Jimmy Luisi was going berserk.

I climbed out of the car and thought, *Boy, what a stunt I did! The director is going to kiss me.*

The director came flying over. "You idiot! You moron!" he screamed. "You'll never do another show for me!"

"Well," I stammered, "did you get it?"

"You were out of range two laps ago," he answered.

While I was staying at Conrad's apartment, I met Ron Samuels, who was struggling to be a manager of entertainers and was pursuing Conrad as a client.

Samuels was married to a beautiful woman named Nancy DeCarl. That's when I first met my wife-to-be. I was not interested at the time, though, because she was married. As I became friendlier with Ronnie, we'd double, go to dinner, and hang out. About a year later, their marriage began to fall apart, and they divorced.

When Nancy became single, we started going out, initially just as friends. There's a saying, "it's better to be friends before you are lovers," and that's what we were. One thing led to another, and what started as a platonic relationship in 1977 resulted in our marriage in 1980, just before *Magnum, P.I.*

However, setting a wedding date and actually getting married was a rocky development. One night we were having dinner with Frank and Barbara Sinatra, and I boldly announced that we would definitely get married. I gave Nancy a firm date, then shifted to several other dates before committing to Valentine's Day. But I got cold feet. The day before the wedding, I told her I was going out for a newspaper and instead got on a plane to Las Vegas. When I returned, she had thrown all my clothes out on the front lawn. At that time, we were living in a little house off Coldwater Canyon.

"It's either do or die," she said.

"Yeah, yeah," I said. "All right."

The next morning, with blood test results in hand, we went to get our marriage license. The ceremony was going to be held at a non-denominational church. Before the ceremony, I told her I was going to the Tail of the Cock, a famous restaurant down the street. All the celebrities, actors, and stars mingled at this place.

"You're not going without me," she insisted, "because you're not taking off again. This is it."

We arrived at the restaurant around four o'clock. I sat at the bar while Nancy went to the ladies room. After ordering drinks, I got up to get a pack of cigarettes. The waitress rushed over to me and said, "Your wife gave me a twenty-dollar bill and told me that if you moved I was to let her know." I sat back down at the bar thinking about Nancy's smart instincts. When I looked up, James Cagney was walking toward me with Rudi Vallee. I leaped out of my seat.

"Mr. Cagney," I stammered, "I hate to bother you..."

"Then why are you, lad?" Cagney retorted.

"Because I'm a big fan and I grew up watching you; and I want to thank you for the tremendous entertainment that you've given me. I'm also an actor."

Rudi Vallee started screaming in my ear, "Don't you know me? I'm Rudi Vallee."

I knew who Rudi Vallee was, and I said, "You're the guy who used to sing through a megaphone."

Nancy returned to the bar.

"We're getting married at five o'clock," I told Cagney. "This is my future wife."

Cagney smiled and congratulated us. He told the bartender to give us drinks.

I had a couple more drinks, and we went over to the church. I didn't bring a witness because Nancy said they had one there. But the guy conducting the service said, "The witness who works here went home early."

"Okay, good," I said. "We'll come back tomorrow."

"No, no," he insisted. "You don't have to do that."

I still tease Nancy about this, telling her that I don't think that we're legally married. Anyhow, the guy married us, wrote down something like "witness not here," and I gave him a hundred-dollar bill. I walked out the front door, went behind a bush, and threw up. I was a wreck. I couldn't believe that I'd actually gotten married, and it took me a few days to get used to the idea.

Sinatra and his wife thought it was cute, especially after I said that I wasn't sure that I was really married because of the lack of a witness.

"I'll get a priest," insisted Frank.

"But Nancy was married before," I said, "and the Catholic Church won't marry us."

"Oh, baloney," he said, "that's nonsense. He'll marry you and we'll have a little reception, but we don't want any press."

It was a thoughtful offer, but we didn't follow through. I figured one wedding was enough for me.

Chapter 3

First Year in Paradise: Nothing but Problems

agnum, P.I. became the third television series to use the Hawaiian islands as its locale. First came *Hawaiian Eye* in the early 1960s, which was really shot in L.A. at Warner Bros. Studios. Then there was *Hawaii Five-O*, the 1970s series starring Jack Lord as police detective Steve McGarrett, which was filmed on location. When *Magnum, P.I.* first started, Lord was clearing out his office at the studio that we took over. I helped him carry his stuff to his car, and he asked me if I wanted to join him at his country club for a snack. I stuck a Lucky Strike in my mouth, and Lord glared at me, removing the cigarette from my mouth. (The guy was a militant non-smoker.) "What, are you nuts?" he asked. "Don't you dare smoke." I found him to be a very kind person. He was the Lord of Hawaii, and his show ran for over a dozen years. *Hawaii Five-O* is still shown in reruns around the world.

Then came *Magnum, P.I.*, and we took over almost right away. The truth is that in the beginning, the star of the show was Hawaii, next it was the red Ferrari, and then it was Selleck. But soon Selleck was labeled "the sexiest man in America." Women used to drop dead over him. They'd tune in, and all they wanted to do was look at Tom. He was also a man's man, and the men would watch to see what he was wearing.

I had just gotten married when I found out that I had a brand new series and was going to Hawaii. Shortly after that, I received the news that my wife, Nancy, was pregnant. Then, within about six months, _Magnum, P.I._ was bulletproof. It was on every magazine cover—the talk of the town. I had a very hard time handling all of this happening at once. I was used to working as an actor, but not being on a megahit show.

Baa Baa Black Sheep was successful for a couple of years, but it wasn't even close to _Magnum, P.I._ in popularity. _Magnum, P.I._ was an icon and is still on TV in reruns. It's one of the biggest shows of all time. They say it was the biggest syndication sale in television history. _Baa Baa Black Sheep_ starred one guy, Robert Conrad, and very few people knew who the rest of us were. But with _Magnum_, there was more than just Selleck. There was also me and Roger Mosley, Tom's buddies from the Vietnam War; and John Hillerman, who played the custodian of the estate. Within a couple of years, _Magnum, P.I._ was a number-one show. I played Tom's best friend, so how could we miss?

But it wasn't smooth sailing right from the beginning. It's never easy starting a show, but our first year on an island paradise brought even more difficulties than I think any of us expected.

First, there was a writers' strike going on when we started, so we pretty much had to "wing" the shows. Everybody was trying to develop their roles, and I was having a really hard time because word came down early on that CBS wasn't happy with my character. They thought I looked way too young to be playing a Humphrey Bogart wannabe. They also thought the character was coming off more like Andy Hardy than a grown-up Vietnam war comrade of Magnum's, running around saying, "Hey, Tom, what are you doing?"

So I wasn't altogether surprised when Don Bellisario called me and said, "Listen, we gotta do something quick or I'm afraid you'll get the ax."

The guy was like a guardian angel to me. He'd beefed up my part on *Baa Baa Black Sheep*, he put me in *Battlestar Galactica*, and now he was going to do his damnedest to keep me as a star in *Magnum, P.I.*

The original premise had Magnum, T. C., and Rick in Vietnam together, Rick as a gunner on a chopper—basically terrified, but unable to admit it. Supposedly, he'd started with the Bogart shtick to cover up this fear. But now the network was down on Rick, saying I did a terrible Bogart—which Bellisario couldn't seem to get across to them was exactly what the character was *supposed* to do. So we had to back down a bit and give up the imitations. But without them, it was tough for me to really define Rick, and the lack of direction showed. With Don's blessing, Selleck suggested a terrific acting coach by the name of Sal Dano, a guy Tom had studied with for eight years. I flew to Los Angeles, and Sal and I sat down over a beer.

53

"Okay," he began, "we start with a bible for your character. Bible says that this man Rick, Orville Wright, came from a broken home, maybe in the Midwest somewhere. Since he left there he always wanted to be recognized. Rick really believed that he was Humphrey—"

"But that's not working," I explained. "They don't like it."

"Well, then, screw it. Bible says your name's Rick. You own your own club. Forget you have any kind of head problems. You're just the guy you are. A guy who walks on both sides of the law. Some chump comes to your back door and says, 'I got fifty hot suits. Give me twenty bucks apiece for them,' you're gonna buy 'em, right?"

I nodded. Sounded okay.

"Fine. But then, next thing you do, you go out and give half the suits to your friends and tell them not to worry about it. That's the kind of guy Rick is. Rick will do anything for his friend, Thomas Magnum. You were in Vietnam together. You were the machine-gunner on a helicopter. A stone-hard killer. You know all about weapons, an expert. A guy who wouldn't blink twice before pulling a trigger and blowing a guy's brains out, then going and eating a sandwich. That's who Rick is."

And that's who Rick became.

It wasn't so much Sal teaching me to act. What he did was to help me find the character of Rick in myself, and it turned out to be a character the network could live with.

"Just be yourself," he said—just like Bellisario had advised me originally. And as the "new" Rick started coming out of his shell, the writers would say, "Hey, that's great." They told me I was naturally funny and then started giving me the funniest lines. They would use me as the tough street guy as well as for comic relief. Eventually Rick's attitude evolved into, "Hey, if you're my friend, you're my friend all the way. But if you mess with me, you're gonna be in the trunk of a Chevy."

Selleck also helped me with the character. He would always give me advice when I had problems, and Don Bellisario was there for me, too. He'd tell me when he felt the scenes were good or when they were a little flat. They, along with Sal Dano, really helped me to develop as an actor, especially as the character, Rick, unfolded.

I had to work hard playing opposite Tom, and I mean that literally. As I said, Tom's six-foot-four and I'm, at the most, five-foot-seven. So, I could either try to stretch myself upwards keeping my head high, which made no sense, or I could do things that showed that size didn't matter. That's what I did. I played Rick as a cocky guy with a certain kind of strut. I would use this technique even off the set. As a matter of fact, one time I was strutting down the street, and I guess I looked a little like a tough guy. Some jerk approached me and asked just how tough I was. I looked at the guy and asked him if he wanted to

Rick, T. C., and Magnum in Rick's club.

find out. He backed off, and thank God for that because in the series, Rick seldom won a fight, and in my life, I didn't win that many either.

Along with dropping the Bogart shtick, we renamed Rick's club from Rick's Café Americain to the King Kamehameha Club (named after the monarch of the island kingdom). One of the things we kicked around after the first year of *Magnum* was that my character would have a seventy-foot yacht at his disposal. It was also going to be named the King Kamehameha. We figured the boat would open up all kinds of story possibilities, and, at one point, the producers thought about doing some underwater action. Tom and I were supposed to get our diving certificates, and, of course, it dawned on me that I was terrified of the water.

We also explored the possibility of having my character be like Charlie Chan's Number One Son from the old movies. He was always messing things up for Charlie Chan and getting in his father's way. This was what we figured Rick could be doing, inadvertently screwing up Tom's investigations and ending up in trouble. It would have provided some good opportunities for comic relief, but we decided to drop it.

〜〜

Shooting a series in Hawaii required that everything be imported: cast, directors, crew, cameras, equipment, motor homes, trucks. And, of course, there were the people who operate the stuff, who also had to be housed and fed. It was like a whole damn army, every day. Universal Studios paid to fly everyone back and forth, not only at the beginning and end of a season, but also at Christmas when we'd take a break and shut down for a couple of weeks. No one wanted to stay in Hawaii over the holidays because our families were back home.

I'll never forget when my son, Lorenzo, was born. My wife, Nancy, called and gave me the news. We had just begun shooting and I was running late for the first scene. I was in such a tizzy that I told her it was great news, and I'd call her back the next chance I got. I raced to the set, and the director said that the crew had received an emergency call and were trying to hunt me down. I told him the call was from my wife, she had just had our baby. "Hell," he said. "What are you, crazy? Go back and call her. We'll wait for you. This doesn't happen every day!"

During production of *Magnum*, my wife and child traveled back and forth from L.A. to Hawaii. When my son started school, and as he got older, it was very difficult for Nancy because she wanted to be there for him. It was very boring in Hawaii for her, and she was an actress, so it was hard for her to sit on the sidelines and watch all this stuff that was going on. She did appear in one episode with me and she was excellent. But for the most part, there was nothing for her to do. We had a small child, too, and I learned something about all of that. I'm no Dr. Spock, but I believe that when a woman has a baby, that becomes her whole life. That's it. You're out. She has a

My wife Nancy is not only beautiful, she's also a terrific actress.

baby, and she wants to take care of her child. We had some problems during this period, and the marriage was a little rocky at times.

Nancy was an actress before we married, and she continued to act some after we were married. She understood the business. I used to get a lot of fan mail from women making me some very interesting offers. Even though they knew I was married, they didn't seem to care. I tried to read all of my fan mail and answer as much as I could, but some of the stuff was really crazy. Nancy got used to it. She was a real sport.

One day, a reporter from one of those nasty little tabloids approached my wife in L.A., saying that she had pictures of me with women coming in and out of my house in Hawaii, as well as on and off of the set of *Magnum*. When you are a celebrity, there are always women hanging around wanting to meet or take pictures with you. The reporter asked my wife whether she was going to divorce me. This is the kind of stuff the tabloids love to do. I called the reporter, enraged, and we threatened each other with all kinds of repercussions. Finally, the reporter agreed to drop the story if I gave her another one to replace it. I obliged and gave her a crazy story about me and extraterrestrials in Hawaii.

I was having trouble adjusting to living in Hawaii, too. I only worked two or three days per episode, and since each episode took about ten days to shoot, I had a lot of time on my hands. I was hitting the Smirnoff a little too much, not to alcoholic status, but somewhat excessively. Being away from my wife so much made me wonder if I should even be married. It was a very difficult period for me. I would never want to go through that again.

I remember once when my wife and son were coming to Honolulu, I hired a Rolls Royce limo to take me to the airport to pick them up. Right before I left my house, the doorbell rang and Robin Leach was standing outside with a six-foot-tall stuffed animal. This was before he became famous as the host of *Lifestyles of the Rich and Famous*. At that time, he was just doing magazine interviews and such. Robin Leach was the kind of guy who would come up and ask, "Tell me, what's going on? Is there any interesting news?" He was a paparazzi guy, sort of like a *National Enquirer* reporter. He was not well known, but I was always nice to everybody, and Robin never forgot it. When I got on *Magnum, P.I.*, and something newsworthy happened, I gave him exclusive inside scoops. That's why he brought the big toy for my kid.

After Robin left, away I went in the Rolls. Ron Masak, the actor who played the policeman on *Murder, She Wrote*, was with me. I remember him telling me, "Go get a bottle of Scope. You smell like a damn brewery."

Back in those days, a lot of actors were heavy drinkers and roustabouts, like John Wayne. Things have changed. Today everybody's into health. But there I was going to the airport in the Rolls, thinking, *Jesus, what am I gonna do with this little kid and wife?* I had this gorgeous house, and I could have had broads swimming around naked in my pool; anything I desired in this tropical paradise. In Hawaii, I was like a big fish in a little pond, but I had a family and I had to be good.

When my family was away, I'd be out until four or five in the morning. I didn't worry about the late hours because I didn't have to wake up until maybe three in the afternoon. Then I'd lay in the steam room and sit in the sun so I'd look good for the evening. I was a playboy, and the show was as hot as a firecracker.

The worst thing that happened during that transitional first year was a freak accident I wish I could forget. We were shooting an action sequence, a scene that required suspending one of our cameramen, Bob Vanderkar, upside down from a helicopter following another helicopter. The choppers were cruising a few feet above the water when suddenly the sea swelled and sent a huge wave smashing into the tail of the first helicopter. It buckled, tossing the cameraman into the sea before crashing seconds later into the water. Even though he'd dislocated his shoulder, the injured pilot, Robert Saunders, tried to find Vanderkar and pull him out. But the cameraman was gone. When police divers found him later, it was clear that he'd died instantly.

It was just awful. Vanderkar was a new crew member who had come to the set right from the airport. After he died we found out that he had brought his pregnant wife with him. It made the whole thing even sadder and, of course, more interesting to the media. The accident was on the front page of all the newspapers in Los Angeles and Hawaii—played so big that I thought it would end the series.

None of us ever forgot that guy. To this day I still think about how that accident could have happened to anyone. We were all in the helicopters from time to time. You just never know.

〰〰

Not long after I arrived in Hawaii I was offered a commercial by a local Porsche dealership. I loved cars and quickly agreed.

"I just have this gut feeling," the owner said, "and I always go with my gut. The show's getting a little attention here, might help me sell a few cars."

So I did the commercial with a 944 Porsche turbo. After the shooting, the owner told me I could drive it for a couple of weeks.

Tom went nuts over it. "Larry, you have to let me sit in it," he said. Of course, what he really wanted to do was drive it. "How about I get you some more lines in the next episode and you loan it to me for a while?"

I tossed him the keys. "It's all yours."

He drove off with a big smile on his face, which was even bigger when he brought it back to the set later that day. "Hang on to it for a bit," I said. "I don't care." I really loved the little Benz I'd had shipped over from L.A.

"Someday," he said, "I'm gonna have one of these. Or better yet, a 928."

"Why's that?"

"Little bigger, little faster. It's top-of-the-line. Maybe you should go back and ask for one."

"They don't think I'm that big a deal, yet," I said. "Maybe someday they'll give me one for keeps."

"Maybe someday I'll be able to afford one for myself and one for everyone in the cast," Tom said.

Of course, we both laughed at that pipe dream. But five years later, when the series was a smash hit, Tom gave every cast member a new Porsche 928.

〰〰

Jeff MacKay, who had been on *Baa Baa Black Sheep* with me and was a good friend, played a recurring character named Mac on *Magnum, P. I.* Mac worked for the Naval Intelligence

Department and was in charge of the computer rooms and records. Magnum used to visit him and con—or somehow coerce—him into divulging information.

Jeff called one evening and asked to borrow the Porsche because he had a date. I said sure. The car only had fifty-six miles on it. Later that night, I heard loud banging on my door. I opened it and Jeff was standing there with no shirt on. On his chest was a big black-and-blue mark that looked like a rope burn.

"What the hell is that?" I asked.

"It's from a seat belt," he answered, "and after you hear what I'm about to tell you, I'll know where our friendship stands and what kind of friend you truly are. I was doing seventy miles an hour and drove straight into a brick wall. I'm lucky I'm alive. The car is now an accordion."

Then he breathed on me and almost melted the features off my face. Jeff liked to have a few tall ones at night, and this night must have been no exception.

The dealer went nuts. "You're never gonna get another car from me," he screamed. But by the third year that *Magnum* was on, when we were a number-one show, the dealer called me again. He asked whether I would do another commercial for them, and promised me another car in exchange. "No," I said, "I think I'm over that."

During that first year, I was living in a condominium right on the ocean at the Colony Surf Hotel. One night I had a party at my place that turned into a crazy scene. There was a lady at the party who had obviously been drinking too much and ingested God only knows what drugs. At about one in the morning, I heard a loud crash in the bathroom. The door was locked so, just like in the movies, I backed up ten feet and charged, full speed, into the door, thinking it would burst open. Instead, I bounced off and dislocated my shoulder.

My friend Tony helped relocate my shoulder, and we both kicked the door down. The lady was on the floor. I was pretty sure she was dead, but to be certain, I called and woke my doctor in Los Angeles and asked how to find vital signs. I followed his instructions and came to the conclusion that this woman, who we did not know, was deader than a doornail. Tony and I dragged her into my bedroom closet and proceeded to be very cool, getting all the people out of the condo.

I sat down, holding my head in my hands. "What are we going to do?" I said. "I can't afford this publicity."

Tony grabbed the woman's feet and I grabbed her arms, and we took her out to the parking lot and placed her underneath a parked car. Then we ran back inside trying to figure out how we could get someone to take her to the hospital.

"Tell you what," I said. "We'll make an anonymous phone call to the police telling them there's a dead girl under a car."

"Won't work," he said. "They're gonna know it's us. First place they're going to come is to your condo because you had a party."

"Yeah, you're right," I said. "Okay, here's what I'm gonna do. I'm gonna call an ambulance."

I dialed the phone. When the emergency operator answered, I said, "We saw this girl crawling around in the parking lot, and she looks as though she's in real deep trouble."

A little while later, we heard the sirens, and the ambulance pulled in. I was watching through the window as the paramedics searched all over, asking people if they had seen an injured person; but they weren't looking underneath any cars.

"What are we going to do?" I asked. "She's under the car, and they're not looking there."

Finally, the paramedics got back in the ambulance and drove away.

"Okay," I said, "we're going to wait until it's light outside and call again."

"Wait a minute," Tony said. "What happens if the guy who owns the car starts it up and runs her over? He's going to think he killed her. This is turning into a nightmare!"

"Screw it." I said. "I'm going to call the hotel switchboard. They'll never know who it is. I'll tell them there's a dead body in the parking lot underneath a car, and hang up."

I called, and this Hawaiian guy answered, "Hello, Colony Surf."

"Excuse me," I whispered, "but there's a dead body underneath a car in the parking lot and you better tend to it right away."

"Under which car, Mr. Manetti?" asked the operator.

"Oh my God!" I screamed.

The switchboard guy met us in the parking lot.

"Listen," I said. "You can't tell anybody that I'm involved. We simply found this body. I'll give you a couple thousand dollars."

We looked under the car and there was no body. The hotel guy thought I was nuts. Tony and I looked at each other, bewildered. Obviously, the woman wasn't dead and had regained consciousness and crawled out. We looked all around, but she was gone.

The next day, the switchboard operator reported me to the condominium association.

After I was politely asked to leave the Colony Surf Hotel, my real estate agent found a great big house with a gorgeous view of the ocean that I rented for $3,500 a month. (This was in the early 1980s. Today it would cost much more.) Nancy flew over with our son, Lorenzo, who at that time was a baby. I rented furniture and had the place set up beautifully.

Our first night in the house, I was sitting in a chair watching television, Nancy was on the sofa, and my son was lying near her playing with a rattle.

"Oh my God!" cried Nancy. "Larry!"

There on the sofa was a spider, and without exaggeration, it was probably at least four inches in diameter. With its legs spread, it appeared to be almost six inches long, and it looked as if it could really hurt someone.

The spider was headed toward my son's head. Nancy reached over and grabbed little Lorenzo just as this thing jumped up and hopped across the living room. It didn't walk like spiders usually do, it hopped like a frog, disappearing as I ran to get a broom. We couldn't sleep all night because of that spider.

The next day, I called the exterminator, told him what had happened, and pleaded with him to come over, find it, and kill it.

"Well," he said calmly, "it's not an 'it.' They're called cane spiders, and if there's one, there are many because they have nests."

I freaked out, called my real estate lady, and told her we were leaving.

"You can't get out of your lease," she insisted.

No one seemed concerned about the giant spiders. We decided to split anyway. We were out of there and into a hotel by the next morning. I had to pay six months rent for one night in the house. I found out later that cane spiders are very docile, harmless, little things. They live in cane fields and eat bugs, and they don't bite. Now they're my friends, but they cost me a fortune: $21,000 for one night. I could have watched Marlin Perkins on *Zoo Parade* and found out about this spider, but I had to learn the hard way.

Chapter 4

With Selleck in Hawaii

O nce the show got underway, Tom and I became pretty close. We took each other's advice most of the time and enjoyed hanging out together—in part because we were so different. I was a high-school dropout from Chicago; Tom was from Southern California, a really bright guy who'd left college only three credits short of a degree.

We'd go out often and have dinner with different people, maybe one of the guest stars or whomever was in town. We frequented Hy's Steak House at first, but eventually got kicked out thanks to some horsing around one night after we'd had a few drinks.

Back then the fashionable thing was eating sushi—raw fish—which I called wild fish. Everybody thought I was nuts. If I saw something that I could get a laugh out of, I'd milk it. There was a fish called Ahi (Ah-he), and Tom had me convinced that there was another fish called A-her. So I'd go in a restaurant and say, "Can I have A-her, please?" The waiter would look at me and ask, "What is that?" I'd say, "You know, I don't want the male fish. I ain't eatin' no male fish. Bring me the female fish. Bring me A-her." Tom would fall to the floor in hysterics, but I played it straight and serious.

I believe that the camaraderie of the costars was very crucial to the success of the show. We would really joke around and carry on with each other, playing every prank imaginable: food fights, cherry bombs, messing with the plentiful insects in Hawaii, exploding cigarettes, and all kinds of crazy things. I remember Tom had a waiter in a restaurant bring me a dessert which turned out to be a dead fish with whipped cream and maraschino cherries on top. Another time, I scooped some bugs out of a bug zapper, sprinkled them on Tom's ice cream, and told him that they were jimmies. He almost ate it, until he noticed that some of the jimmies were moving.

Many of the cast and crew members worked out at the Honolulu Club. Tom stayed fit there and often visited after playing volleyball. I dried out there occasionally after a night of carousing. Selleck and I would bump into each other pretty often, usually in the steam room. Tom looked at me one afternoon and said, "Larry, you're supposed to earn the steam room. It's a reward after you work out."

"Oh," I responded, "doesn't it count for being rewarded for the night before? I'm depositing about sixty dollars worth of vodka."

One evening, Tom and I were dining at an Italian restaurant and my attempt to liven things up went a bit too far. There was a Hawaiian Tropic convention in town, and five or six of their "Suntan Girls" came over to ask for our autographs. Sometimes fans would only ask for Tom's, which burned me a little, but these girls wanted both of ours and it felt great.

Before I knew it, Tom—unmarried at the time—had asked them to join us. They took a few pictures with us, then sat down, and we all ordered dinner and drinks. It was fun at first, but after an hour or so, and three or four rounds, it was pretty clear that we'd run out of things to talk about. I looked over and saw Tom just sitting there twisting his mustache, staring at the ceiling.

I kicked him under the table and asked what was wrong.

"I'm bored," he responded.

"*Bored?*" I said. "I can fix that."

I pulled out a Baretta .22 automatic I had just bought and happened to be carrying, aimed it straight up, and emptied the clip into the ceiling. At eight o'clock on a Friday night, the place was jumping; everybody ducked when they heard the shots. Then the owner, a swarthy Italian guy, came rushing over—to kill me, I figured.

"Give me another clip," was all he said.

He put his hand out for the gun and I gave it to him, half wondering if I had better duck in a hurry. Before I knew it, he had a row of empty beer cans set up on the bar.

"Watch this!" he said as he shot a couple of cans off of the bar. He handed me the gun and motioned for me to try.

Why not? I thought.

I shot a can off, but by that point the place was going bananas, and the girls we'd been eating with were petrified. Tom got up and grabbed hold of me, no longer bored.

"We're leaving," he ordered. "Right now, before the cops get here!"

There are still bullet holes in the ceiling of that restaurant to this day.

Selleck and I opened a 365-seat restaurant in 1986 called the Black Orchid. It was gorgeous. We had superstars like Liza Minnelli, Sammy Davis Jr., and Frank Sinatra dine there when they were performing in Hawaii. It was one of the most prestigious restaurants to ever open in Honolulu.

One year, we grossed ten million dollars. That's unheard of for a restaurant. Tom donated memorabilia, pictures, all kinds of stuff from *Magnum, P.I.* It took almost an hour to walk around and view all the mementos in the restaurant. People would come to eat just so they could look around. It was an expensive place to dine, and Tom realized that a lot of people couldn't afford to go there. We opened for lunch with inexpensive fare so that these people could visit. We lost money doing this, but that was the kind of guy Tom was.

"Let everybody come in so they can look around," he said, "and if they want to order a Coke and a hamburger, that's fine."

We opened the Black Orchid because we used to hang out in different joints all over town, and we wanted our own place. We didn't put up any of our own money, though, just our names. And our names brought in that kind of revenue. After we grew unhappy with the management of the restaurant and got out of the deal, the place went bankrupt within one year.

The final straw came about in a funny way. Tom and I had what we'd call "unlimited comps." We could treat anyone to anything in the place.

One day, I phoned the restaurant manager and asked, "How many cases of champagne do you have?"

He replied, "We've got seven cases of Cristal and eight cases of Dom."

Then I asked, "How many ounces of caviar?" And he told me. "Listen," I ordered, "there's a lot of important people coming into town tonight. Double it."

Now, Tom wasn't involved in this little fiasco, but I was.

On Friday and Saturday night, when the Mr. and Mrs. Smiths from Iowa sat down at their tables, I sent them an ounce of caviar and a bottle of Cristal. I just gave it away. I did this for as many customers as I could. The bill was over $15,000, and I signed off on it. At the bottom of the check I wrote, "Aloha, it was a great time while it lasted."

In the middle of our eight-year run on *Magnum*, I decided that I wanted to go onstage and sing. It had been something that I

Lon Bently (far right), our makeup man on Magnum, *kept us all looking good.*

had dreamed of even before I wanted to be an actor. So I hooked up with Jimmy Halvah and Ron Douglas. Halvah was one of the lead singers and writers for a group called the Buccaneers, and he wrote songs like "Kind of a Drag." He and Douglas came up with three or four original tunes for me. (Ron Douglas was in the news recently; he was the friend that Brynn Hartman went to after she killed her husband Phil, and before she killed herself.)

I went to a singing instructor to tune-up my vocal skills. Then I went to CBS Records and was told that if I came up with an album, they'd produce it. I recorded four great tunes. I'm not saying I was great, but the tunes were great.

Lon Bently, the makeup artist on *Magnum, P.I.*, invited Selleck, Carol Burnett, Nancy, and one or two other couples to dinner at his place one night. We were at this long table, talking and listening to music, when I thought to myself, *Gee, this sounds familiar.*

Then I realized it was me singing. Ron looked over at me and mouthed, "Shut up. Don't say anything."

He told the group, "This is a new guy. How do you like him?"

"Gosh," answered Tom, "this is a great tune. I like it."

Then Carol Burnett chirped in, "This guy is very good!"

I figured this had to be a put-on. But after the third song, I could tell that they really enjoyed it and didn't know it was me.

When Ron turned the tape off, he announced, "Guess what? That was Larry."

Tom was wide-eyed. "If you need any help," he told me, "I'll be there."

The tape was sent to Las Vegas, and the Frontier Hotel called me with an offer of $35,000 a week for eight weeks. I agreed and flew into Vegas with Ron Douglas and Peter Terranova, who was then vice president of Universal Studios.

I walked into the showroom of the hotel, and there was Freddy Fender with his name in lights, and twelve people in the audience. I figured if Freddy Fender had only twelve people in this room which seated fifteen hundred, I was in big trouble. So I turned around and I started walking out of the showroom. This little man yelled out, "Where are you going?"

"Woodland Hills," I answered.

I hailed a cab and checked in to Caesar's Palace. Peter and Ron met me there. We partied and I let off all my steam. When I returned to L.A., I was slapped with a lawsuit for $180,000 from the Frontier. I settled since I never went on stage.

Abandoning my chance at a singing career is one of my great regrets to this day, and I think if I had another opportunity I'd try again.

~~~

When *Magnum* became very popular, I began to receive calls from studios and production companies offering me great roles, pilots, and other series. The hook was that I'd be given a

With Tom and his wife, Jillie Mack.

great role *only* if I could convince Tom to be in the project, too. I didn't think that was right. I was very loyal to Tom, and I would never go behind his back and do something like that. I also didn't want to spend my career riding on Tom's coattails. I lost a lot of work because I refused to exploit my relationship with Selleck.

Occasionally, my wife Nancy and I had dinner with Tom and his then-girlfriend, Jillie Mack. The gossip reporters, paparazzi, and tabloids were always bothering me, trying to get me to say things about Tom and his relationship with Jillie and other women, but I wouldn't touch it. I warned them never to put my name in any kind of rumormongering tabloid story about Tom.

There were times when I would look at the hours that Tom put in and think to myself, I don't ever want to be a lead in a series and go through what Tom is going through. I could see how it sometimes took its toll on him. And then, in the show's seventh year, three out of the first four episodes featured my character, Rick. Like Tom, I was putting in those ten to fifteen hours a day, six days a week, and I realized that it was tough, but not as bad as I thought it would be. Then I told myself that when *Magnum, P.I.* ended, if I ever got the shot to be a series lead, I would. It hasn't happened yet.

Chapter 5

The Real Selleck

think Tom's parents can be credited with why he is so well-adjusted. They raised him right. He told me they weren't strict but instead led by example. They were great role models for Tom, his sister, and two brothers. Tom was an athlete who went to USC on a basketball scholarship. His first job was a Pepsi commercial, and he later appeared on *The Dating Game*. He didn't even get the girl.

Tom was in the 1970 movie *Myra Breckinridge* with the great actress Mae West. There was gossip that Mae actually uttered her famous quote, "Come up and see me sometime," to him. According to Tom, she always said that to good-looking men because she didn't wake up until late.

Tom also appeared on the soap opera *The Young and the Restless*, and acted in a few films, although he only admits to two of them.

In addition, Selleck did a couple of TV pilots. Shortly before *Magnum*, he costarred with Robert Urich in a pilot called *Bunco*. The network rejected the series, saying that between the two of them, they didn't have enough presence to carry the series. Can you believe that?

The good life: Sharing stogies and stories with an old friend.

One of the ways Tom supplemented his income during the lean years was posing for Salem cigarette billboard advertisements. It was ironic, because Tom never smoked cigarettes. (Today, however, he does puff an occasional cigar.)

Quite a few Hollywood types felt that a lot of Tom's success was due to his role in the TV movie *The Sacketts*, a Louis L'Amour western that aired on NBC shortly before Tom's contract with Universal was about to expire.

There's a great Hollywood story in how Selleck actually came within twenty-four hours of not doing *Magnum, P.I.* at all. When Universal Studios committed him to do the *Magnum* pilot, he was already under contract for a series called *Boston and Kilbride*. Since that show was passed over by the networks, Selleck figured that was the end of his commitment to Universal. But he hadn't really read the fine print and ended up having to sign on to do *Magnum* on the 364th day of the contract's final year. Tom wasn't happy about it at first, because as I mentioned before, his character in the original *Magnum* pilot was not the kind of guy he wanted to play. Tom even thought about suing Universal to get out of the show, because he felt he had already fulfilled his commitment to them. But after Don Bellisario rewrote the pilot, Tom felt a lot better about the character, and decided to do the show.

A few months earlier, Tom had done a television movie-of-the-week called *Concrete Cowboys*. Everyone thought it would get picked up for a series, and here he was, obligated to the *Magnum* show. His part in *Cowboys* was recast, and a few episodes were made with a different star. If you include *Magnum*, Tom did seven pilots, five of which bombed.

Before *Magnum* was scheduled to begin shooting, Tom was offered the lead in the Steven Spielberg movie *Raiders of the Lost Ark*. Sensing a big hit, he went to Universal and asked for a later start-up date for *Magnum* so he could do the movie. But Universal couldn't accommodate him. Tom wasn't thrilled at missing a starring role in a big feature film for the sake of a chancy TV series, but he didn't do what thousands of actors would have done—make the film, screw the studio, and let them sue. He honored his obligation and never complained, even when the movie became a megahit and made Harrison Ford a superstar.

~~~

There were rumors that Selleck dumped his first wife, Jackie, after *Magnum* became successful, but that wasn't the case. They were separated at least six months before we shot the pilot for Magnum, and during that first year, they were having rough times. Tom had raised her son like his own, and he felt sad about how the breakup would affect the boy.

Success kept Tom from going out in public very often. He had to stop driving his red Ferrari because it was like waving a flag. Everybody wanted to either scream, jump out at him, or pull up alongside. Tom had to sneak into movies after they had begun and could only go to McDonald's with his stepson during off-hours.

This lack of privacy really bugged Tom as the years went by. The success of *Magnum* even changed the lives of his family. His parents and siblings often received calls at three or four in the morning from a magazine or tabloid wanting to know if there was any truth to various rumors about Tom. They had to make adjustments to their lives, too.

Tom actually had trouble getting dates during the early years of *Magnum*. You would think a great-looking guy like Selleck would never have a problem, but a lot of women didn't want to go out with him because they were afraid they would end up on the gossip pages the next day. Tom talked about this fact in an interview in *Playboy* magazine in December 1983.

Selleck was very low-key and did not aggressively pursue women. And believe me, if he had been a womanizer, it would have caught up with him while we were in Hawaii. He could have had a lot of problems with boyfriends or jealous husbands, but nothing like that ever occurred. Working six days, eighty hours a week, he never actually had time to get involved in any serious relationships when we were filming *Magnum*. Even though he could have used his clout to lighten his load on the show, he never took advantage of that. He put in longer hours than anyone else, even to the detriment of his personal life.

Don Bellisario spun an anecdote about two stewardesses he met on a plane when he was flying to Hawaii. Each one independently gave him a bottle of champagne, begging him to be sure he shared it with Tom. Bellisario told me that it totally deflated his ego.

In order to find out what made the series and Selleck tick, Bellisario conferred with a consultant whom Universal hired to survey audiences as to what they liked or disliked about *Magnum, P. I.* The survey found that people liked an open mystery; they wanted to discover clues the way Thomas Magnum did. The survey also revealed that people didn't care if Magnum's clients were sympathetic, or if every story had a happy ending.

Additionally, the survey revealed that the most devoted viewers were women between the ages of eighteen and forty-five. Surprisingly, men liked the show despite the fact that Selleck turned on their girlfriends and wives. To men, he was a likeable, vulnerable kind of guy who was attractive in a non-threatening way. Most guys would have huge egos if they looked like Selleck, but he was not really affected by his good looks.

I can't tell you how many times somebody walked up to me and said, "My boyfriend looks exactly like Tom Selleck," or "My husband is Tom Selleck's twin." The truth is that these guys manufactured themselves to look like Tom. I would often see red Ferraris pass by with the tops down, driven by guys in Hawaiian shirts and mustaches. I've seen this in different cities around the world. I used to crack up and pinch myself, thinking, *I'm a part of this show where all these people are trying to emulate the star!*

And there was nothing wrong with that because I always had an idol or mentor while I was growing up. I couldn't think of a better guy for young people to emulate than Tom Selleck.

Tom was a team player who played volleyball frequently in Hawaii. He played with ex-Olympic athletes at the exclusive Oahu Outrigger Canoe Club. His team won their way to Texas to compete in the Over-35 Senior Tourney, finishing second in the 1981 national championships. Selleck was also named to the All-American Honorable Mention Team along with two of his teammates.

A team player on *Magnum, P.I.*, too, Selleck went to the "mat" for the cast and crew. One time, we were filming a show directed by Burt Kennedy on the other end of the island. Burt had directed John Wayne in many films, mostly westerns. I was very excited that Kennedy was there.

It rained every day, and we couldn't catch a break. I was cooped up in a room. When the sun finally came out, we still weren't filming, and that was unusual. Then I found out that

Tom had taken off for L.A. over some production issues in the show. He was a stickler for putting all the dollars on the screen and not wasting money, and he had grown frustrated over the past two episodes. When he took this time off, he refused his salary for those days, even though the studio tried to pay him. "Don't worry about it," insisted one of Universal's corporate VP's, "it's all straightened out. Take the money."

Selleck would not touch it.

〜〜〜

As *Magnum, P. I.* took off and made Selleck a household name, he received countless offers for movie roles and other projects. Toward the end of our second year, Joseph Papp, the big-time Broadway producer, approached him about doing a month's run of the hit show, *Pirates of Penzance*. Kevin Kline was performing in it at the time. It was a good macho role for Tom, but as it turned out, he wasn't available to do it because *Magnum* was ready to begin filming again. I thought that was just as well, since I couldn't picture Tom in a Broadway musical.

Tom's first big feature film was *High Road to China* in 1983. The premiere was in the grand old Hollywood tradition: big search lights, red carpets, top celebrities, and stretch limos. Even though I'd been in Hollywood for years, I had never been to the world premiere of a movie, let alone invited and flown in at the expense of the star. Tom flew Roger, John, and me in, and also paid for our hotel rooms and meals.

It was a real high for me, and after the screening, Tom invited the cast of *Magnum, P. I.* to join him for pictures and the reception. In no way was Tom looking to gain publicity for himself or even the show. It was just his way of including his friends in his happiness and success.

One thing that was especially great about working with Tom was the fact that he appreciated his cast and crew as few stars do. In our fifth year, he had three Porsche 928s delivered as a surprise to me, Roger Mosley, and John Hillerman at our

The cast with Selleck when he received his star on the Hollywood Walk of Fame. Tom always included his costars in his success.

79

homes. And during the last season, he gave out solid-gold Rolex watches to producers, casting people, and a few crew members. The rest of the *Magnum, P.I.* family—well over a hundred people—got regular Rolex watches, some custom-made with the *Magnum* logo.

Tom hadn't even gone for a wholesale deal on those watches. He wanted the money he paid to benefit the state of Hawaii, so he'd gone into jewelry stores all over Honolulu and bought as many as they had.

Bonuses came out of his own pocket, too. Anyone who worked on the show got a bonus, and he threw the biggest party the island had ever seen, which easily cost tens of thousands of dollars.

All told, the watches, money, gifts, and parties easily amounted to over half a million dollars. That kind of generosity is very unusual for a TV star—I've never heard of anything like it. With some stars, you're lucky if they send you a basket of fruit when it's over.

At the end of the series, we were given the *Magnum* ring to keep. On the gift package that Selleck had made for me, it said: "French cross ring worn by Orville Wright, *Magnum, P.I.*" Orville Wright was the real name of my character. When I opened the gift, there was a ring box inside, and it was empty, except for a piece of paper with the words: "Stolen by Larry Manetti, 1989."

~~~

One afternoon, I caught up with Tom just as he was getting into a limo, looking dapper as hell.

"Hey, where you going?" I asked him.

"I wish I could take you," he said, "but it wouldn't be proper."

"Proper? Why? Who're you going to see? And in a *limo*?"

Tom grinned. "Just the President of the United States."

I patted him on the back and told him I wanted to hear everything when he got back. Tom was more than happy to oblige.

"It was great!" he said when he returned. "Reagan's still pretty well on top of what's happening in television and in the movies, you know. We bullshitted all afternoon about Hollywood politics."

"What did you drink?" I asked.

"Coors beer."

"And Reagan?"

"Smirnoff and orange juice."

"Russian vodka? That's like smoking a Cuban cigar!"

"Tom," I continued, hesitantly, "did he by any chance mention me at all?"

"How'd you know?" Tom answered with a laugh. "He said if he were still head of the Screen Actors Guild, you'd never have gotten your SAG card."

(Tom's taken a lot of liberal Hollywood heat over the past dozen years for his conservative leanings and his staunch support of Republican politicians such as Reagan and Bush. There's even been talk of Selleck running for office—but I don't see it. He's just a guy with very strong beliefs in individualistic solutions. I know for a fact he even supported liberal types like Paul Tsongas and Jerry Brown.)

Another time, Tom was invited to the White House for a dinner honoring Prince Charles and Princess Di. A lot of people felt that Tom was invited because of his support for Reagan, but actually the invitation came from the English officials—either Charles or Di were great fans of Selleck. I like to think they were great fans of *Magnum* and just accidentally left me off of the invitation list.

~~~

Sometimes Tom would get so frustrated at negative pieces written by journalists and columnists that he would actually hold mini press conferences to set the record straight. In the summer of 1985, there was an article written that basically said that Selleck had lost his mass appeal and that he, and the show, were on the decline. Tom told the reporters who gathered with him over breakfast at the Colony Surf, a beach front restaurant in Waikiki, that *all* he did that year was win an Emmy as best dramatic actor on TV, receive a Golden Globe Award, and win two People's Choice awards (he won as favorite male TV performer, and tied for favorite all-around male entertainer with Eddie Murphy). He hosted the Emmy Awards and cohosted the Oscars. Some decline.

In June 1986, Tom earned a star on Hollywood Boulevard's Walk of Fame. He brought the entire cast in for the ceremony, and we joined him for photos when the star was uncovered.

This was, however, a frustrating period for Tom. We were going up against Bill Cosby's show, which was just about the hottest series ever on TV. Since the network didn't want to move us to a different time slot, we had the toughest position on television and we were really feeling the heat.

There were close to two hundred people working on *Magnum, P.I.* in one capacity or another, and we didn't want to see anyone lose their job. Rumors were rampant that the show was going to be canceled, and it really affected everybody in terms of morale.

We were doing everything we could to upgrade the quality of the scripts and the production values. Universal was spending one and a half million dollars per episode in Hawaii at that time, which greatly benefited the economy of the state and provided a lot of jobs. Tom was very bugged about the rumors. He said, "Look, this is my hometown as much as anybody else's. These rumors are unfounded and cruel."

Everyone was ready to bury us in 1986, but all of a sudden, around the middle of 1987, we were a rising television show again. The press wrote about the "resurgence of *Magnum, P.I.*" However, we felt that we had always had a strong following.

But this was a period when everybody was taking potshots at Tom. The critics were knocking his movies, but I don't think that Tom owed anyone an apology. I saw every one of his movies and they were all good. They were all profitable, and people don't realize that less than 5 percent of all movies ever make money.

There were a number of articles reporting Tom's salary and exaggerating it. Each time the story was picked up on radio, TV, or the newspapers, the salary kept increasing. By the time we arrived to do a *Magnum* episode in London, rumors had Tom's salary at over $5,000,000 more than he was actually making.

Tom took it in stride. He never felt guilty about making so much money. It wasn't at anyone else's expense, and he wasn't hiding it under his mattress. He spent it. The more money he

You couldn't ask for a better or more generous friend than Tom Selleck.

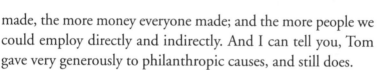

made, the more money everyone made; and the more people we could employ directly and indirectly. And I can tell you, Tom gave very generously to philanthropic causes, and still does.

At the end of our shooting schedule in 1987, Tom took out a $6,500 full-page ad in the *Honolulu Star Bulletin* and *Honolulu Adviser* thanking the residents of Hawaii for the best seven years of his life. He wanted to reach as many people as he could to show his appreciation, and he wanted to thank everybody for their cooperation and for respecting his privacy. The same week there was a State House Resolution presented to us by the Republican representative, Barbara Marumoto, which honored the entire crew of *Magnum*. During the presentation, she said that Tom had told her that the cast always receives laurels when in fact it's everybody involved in the show who creates a truly successful television series.

At the start of our seventh season, Tom successfully lobbied the network for a better time slot, and we ended up beating out

Dynasty on Wednesday nights. It was a smart move that boosted the hell out of our ratings.

After that, Tom started taking a much bigger role in the production of the series, even becoming executive producer of the show for its last year or so. He helped develop scripts, assisted in the editing process, and recruited big guest stars. He was putting in far too many hours each week, but it certainly paid off where the quality of the show was concerned.

The start of our eighth season found Tom newly married to Jillie. He also turned up on the list of the twenty-five highest paid entertainers in *Forbes* magazine. He tied with ex-Beatle Paul McCartney. Both were far behind Bill Cosby, who came in first with an income of about 84 million dollars in the prior two years.

Near the end of the 1980s, Tom didn't want to do *Magnum, P.I.* anymore—even though the ratings were still strong. He had a seven-year contract and the seven years were up. After working so hard on the series while also doing several movies simultaneously, he needed a rest. Everyone wanted him to stay on, so he generously agreed to do another thirteen episodes.

It was nice because in the end, *Magnum* was never canceled. It was Tom's choice to stop. Who knows, if he'd wanted to keep on with the show it might still be on the air.

Actually, every year, I thought that *Magnum* would be canceled, but I'm that way. I never believed anything good was going to last. I always thought that a black cloud was going to arrive. I was on other series that were dropped. I was on *Baa Baa Black Sheep*, *The Duke*, and *Battlestar Galactica*. These were good shows with decent ratings, and they got killed.

Jeff Sagansky, then president of CBS, called me a couple of years ago and said, "I'll guarantee six two-hour *Magnum* movies for the cast. We can play two a year, one a year, three a year, whatever you want; or we'll give you an order for another series."

I was thrilled, of course, that the network still felt so strongly about us.

"I can't talk to you about this," I said. "You know it's not my decision."

Sagansky begged me to convince Selleck, but Tom wanted a full-length *Magnum* feature film in the theaters or nothing. No more TV *Magnum*. I could see his point. With a feature film budget, we could have done amazing things.

That was almost three years ago, and, with the continuing popularity of our syndicated TV series, the possibility of a *Magnum* movie is still very much alive.

Chapter 6

Guest Stars and Celebrity Visitors

O ur audience appreciated the numerous guest performers we had on the show—many of them real superstars. We didn't need to seek them out—they liked the show and wanted to do it. The budget didn't allow for paying most stars what they were worth. Frank Sinatra, for instance, could pull in a quarter of a million dollars for a week's work. We paid him $2,500. But he was a big fan of the show, and it was easy to convince him to do an episode. I was thrilled at the prospect of working with him, but had no idea how crazy his presence would make things.

When the filming started, it was total pandemonium. There were mobs of people everywhere, and we needed dozens of extra security guards to keep the crowds at bay. I guess Frank got a little fed up with it because as I was about to go into makeup one afternoon, an arm came around and grabbed me.

"Come on. We're going to dinner." It was Sinatra and a limousine driver, the biggest Hawaiian I had ever seen in my life. "Where's this Italian joint you guys go to all the time?"

We managed to get away unnoticed and headed over to Sergio's. But it was early, only four-thirty in the afternoon, so

Frank did things his way! And what fun it was to be along for the ride.

the restaurant wasn't open yet. I walked in with Sinatra, and the maitre d' turned stark white.

"Sergio, God's here!" he yelled. "Jesus Christ is here! *Francesco*, he's here!"

Sergio trotted out from the kitchen and almost dropped to the floor. Sinatra and I sat down, and we ordered fried calamari, a few different appetizers, and a couple of Jack Daniels. Sinatra hit it off immediately with Sergio and soon we were eating like kings and having a ball. We were there almost two hours, and the next thing I knew, the director and producer of the episode were calling on the phone, asking for me.

"What, are you guys crazy?" they were both on the line screaming at me. "What the hell are you doing?"

"Sinatra called dinner," I answered.

"Dinner!" the director shouted. "Sinatra called dinner? But we didn't call dinner! Get your asses back here!"

That was Sinatra, though. He was hungry. That was it. He did things his way.

You hear a lot of stories about what a perfectionist Sinatra was when he was doing a scene, and they're all true. Although Frank prefers one take, he wants it to be right, and if somebody is not doing a good job, he's going to let them know. We were shooting a big fight scene and Frank insisted on doing his own stunts. We rehearsed it seven or eight times. It was one of those situations that had to be precise or someone could get hurt. Sinatra was in his seventies at the time, recovering from an operation, and awaiting another one.

"Let's go," said Frank as he looked at me and winked. "Get a picture of this."

I stood up on a table with a Polaroid Instamatic flash camera. The crew had three cameras. "All right," shouted the director, "A camera, B camera, C camera, action." The fight scene began. I snapped the picture in the middle of the scene and my flash went off. The director yelled, "Cut! A camera, B camera, C camera!"

The assistant director screamed, "Did you get it?"

"No," said one of the cameramen. "Someone took a picture, there's a flash in it."

They all turned around and looked at me, and I lied, "It wasn't me." But just then my camera made that distinctive whirring noise, and out popped an instant photo of Frank punching a guy. They wanted to kill me.

"Frank told me to do it," I confessed.

"Give me the picture," interrupted Frank. "All right, we'll do it again. Let's go."

The director and the cameramen smiled. They didn't want to mess with Frank.

In the episode, Sinatra played a detective who came to Hawaii to pursue an elusive criminal. Now this is no secret, but about twenty-five years ago, Frank had hair transplants. Unfortunately, they didn't grow in very well, so he wore a small hairpiece on the front of his head. While he was doing the

Sinatra in action. This is the photo that got me in trouble.

Magnum episode, he left the hairpiece off, and it looked as if the transplants were shrinking back. When the publicity pictures of Frank were sent out, somehow or another the photos got screwed up and the images were distorted. He looked much more bald than he actually was. I know it was rather upsetting for Frank when these black and white pictures ended up in *USA Today*.

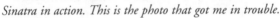

There was a scene in one episode where Carol Burnett, Tom, and I were walking into a building. It was a very serious scene—she was supposed to be on the verge of crying. Unbeknownst to me, they had set me up. Tom had told Carol that I was afraid of bugs.

When I walked into the scene, which we had already rehearsed, I was supposed to shake Tom's hand. They were ready to shoot, and I saw that Carol, who's such a good actor, already had real tears in her eyes. I shook Tom's hand and there was a cockroach in it that crawled into my hand. I screamed, "Ah, shit!"

"How could you ruin the scene?!" Tom yelled. They busted my chops. Tom was a great practical joker.

Ernie Borgnine did an episode and I wanted to impress him because I had grown up idolizing him. I invited him to dinner, and he accepted. I rented a stretch limousine, and pulled up in front of his hotel around eight o'clock to pick him up.

"What's this for?" he asked.

"We're going to dinner."

"Cut this guy loose," he said, referring to the driver. "We're taking a cab."

He wouldn't get into the limo. We went to dinner in a cab, and he split the check with me.

Another incident with Ernie involved the director's chairs that the stars sat on before each scene. Every time we moved from one scene to the next, Borgnine picked up his chair and

Carol Burnett, a great friend and a funny lady.

On Magnum, *I got to work with some of my childhood idols, like Ernie Borgnine.*

carried it himself. He was a terrific guy. He sang opera to us, and he was very, very bright, not to mention one of the nicest men that I've ever met in my life.

～～～

Carol Channing came to Hawaii to be a guest star on *Magnum* playing herself. I knocked on her dressing room door, and when she opened it, I said, "Hello, Dolly."

"I like that," she said. "What's your name?"

I introduced myself and we chatted for a few minutes. She told me that it was very special to her that I had come over to introduce myself since a lot of actors, over the years, had been very snobbish.

A couple of years later, while I was still doing *Magnum*, Carol and Betty White were doing what is called a fifteen-minute test for a sitcom. Miss Channing remembered me and requested that the producer put me in the test. I was very honored. Unfortunately, it didn't sell. However, when I saw her again I said, "Hello, Dolly."

~~~

In one of our flashback shows set in Vietnam, Joe Moore, a good actor and newscaster in Honolulu, was our guest star. After we finished his scene, I told Joe that he looked too clean to be playing a guy who was in Vietnam in a rainstorm. So I made a big mud pie and threw it smack in his face. Then he made one and threw it at me. I threw one at Roger Mosley, and a huge mud-pie fight commenced. When we were done, everyone was covered in mud.

A local newsman heard third-hand about the mud fight and incorrectly reported that the cast of *Magnum* was embroiled in an argument that led to a physical altercation and resulted in the mud fight. It was picked up by the international news wires and reported all over the world.

~~~

I first met Jose Ferrer when he was in a *Magnum, P.I.* episode with his son, Miguel, June Lockhart, and her daughter, Annie Lockhart. Jose and I hit it off tremendously well. We'd go out to dinner and he would tell me all those wonderful old stories about Hollywood. I got him into the Wild Eye Golf Course because he loved to play golf. Later he sent me all kinds of articles and little gifts. I realized that he was one of the special ones in the entertainment industry. Ferrer was old Hollywood, very sincere, and a truly nice man.

~~~

Dick Butkus came to Hawaii to do an episode. One day, Dick and I were watching a football game with my friend Fred Piluso when my macaw parrot began to scream.

"Shut up, shut up!" I yelled at the macaw.

"I'll tell you what," said Butkus. "There is one way to shut this parrot up."

He picked up the cage, walked out on my balcony, turned the cage upside down, and the parrot flew away.

That night, we all went out and got blasted. We returned to my place with a bunch of people. I started lighting cherry bombs and throwing them at Butkus and Piluso. They were exploding all over my apartment. Then Butkus started heaving them off the balcony.

Later, we had a contest to see who could throw a cherry bomb the farthest before it blew up. After we were finished with that, the guys threw all of my underwear off the balcony.

The next day, there was an eviction notice taped to my front door. I went to the management office and swore I had nothing to do with the cherry-bomb incident.

"It must have been another apartment," I reasoned. "The tattler's vision was off."

"Then whose are these?" asked the manager, holding up a pair of my shorts labeled "Larry Manetti."

〰〰〰

Dennis Weaver, whose credits include *McCloud, Gentle Ben, Gunsmoke,* and many other TV shows and films, was another guest star. He was also a songwriter who played the guitar and sang. His son, Rick Weaver, was one of our producers for several years.

〰〰〰

Magnum, P.I. was a springboard for many actors. Sharon Stone, Dana Delany, and Ted Danson were among a slew of then-unknown guest stars. Sometime after Danson's guest appearance, Don Bellisario did a pilot called *Tales of the Gold Monkey.* The studio and Bellisario wanted Danson to star. Unfortunately, Ted was an unknown at that point, and the ABC network demanded Stephen Collins, an actor who was more recognizable than Danson. So poor, rejected Ted Danson went on to take a pilot called *Cheers.*

Shannen Doherty, who was only a child at the time, was in an episode where Roger Mosely had to go into a boxing ring and fight. I know that she received some bad press during *Beverly Hills, 90210*, but when she did our show, she was a perfect little lady who did a great job, too.

~~~

My wife Nancy acted with me in a *Magnum* episode called "Computer Date" where this gentleman hired Magnum to find out who was committing computer espionage. He also asked Magnum to investigate the strange behavior of his wife, played by Nancy, who he believed was having an affair. Magnum reluctantly agreed and was shocked when he discovered that the wife's alleged lover was none other than my character, Rick.

Nancy did a terrific, unbelievable job. However it was very difficult for me. When I thought about her role and put myself in the position of the suspicious husband, I was perplexed. When you think about your wife having an affair, strange things go through your mind. Nancy was so good at it that I wondered if she actually *was* having an affair.

Everyone was extremely impressed with Nancy's acting ability. Most didn't know that she was a child actress and had been in movies and television for years.

At six years old, Nancy danced with Donald O'Connor in the movie *Anything Goes*. From there, it was appearances in numerous western series, including *The Rifleman, Cheyenne, Gunsmoke,* and *Wagon Train*.

Along with several other children, Nancy sang "High Hopes" with Frank Sinatra in a TV special. She was Paul Petersen's first girlfriend on *The Donna Reed Show*.

Nancy was in *Bye, Bye, Birdie* and several other movies including a scene with the late, great character actor J. T. Walsh in *Wired—The John Belushi Story*.

Tom's first wife, Jackie Ray, and my wife, Nancy, both grew up in the San Fernando Valley and were friends from high school. Ironically, they each appeared in a *Magnum, P.I.* episode.

I had a boyhood friend named Michael Spilotro whose family name was frowned upon in organized crime enforcement circles. There was the role of an FBI agent in one *Magnum* episode, and I asked Michael, who was visiting Hawaii, if he would like to play this role.

Spilotro said, "Geez, I'd love it."

So Michael played the role in a scene where he went into a warehouse with a megaphone and projected his voice to these gangsters. "This is the FBI. Get up against the wall!" Then he handcuffed and arrested them.

At the end of the show, the credits read, "FBI Agent... Michael Spilotro." I bet the FBI went nuts.

As the show's popularity grew, so did the number of celebrities who visited the set while they were in Hawaii. Some were just vacationing, some actually lived there, and some came to entertain.

We were filming a scene on the beach one afternoon when all of a sudden I heard a bunch of hushed gasps. Burt Reynolds had come to the set to visit Tom and wish him good luck. A few weeks later he sent Tom a sarcastic letter accusing him of stealing his mustache. Around 1981, Burt started saying that Tom was his clone. Later, Tom's production company produced Burt's TV show, *B. L. Stryker*.

Of course, the stars who visited us on the *Magnum* set weren't all the big-time, movie-variety like Burt. We also had Billy Joel, Bob Hope, and the Everly Brothers. We even had Gabe Kaplan from *Welcome Back, Kotter*. Sylvester Stallone and Burt Reynolds both had homes in Hawaii. In those days Burt lived next to Jim Nabors and Carol Burnett. Anybody who was somebody would drop by, especially when we were shooting on the beach.

Anthony Quinn seemed like instant family.

Anthony Quinn, a tremendous fan of Tom's, came to visit us on the set two or three times. He took Tom and I to dinner with his kids, and we had a wonderful time. Quinn asked me to read for the producers of a Broadway play he was doing. He flew me to New York to audition. When I got on stage, there was a light bulb hanging in front of my face, and I asked Anthony, "What do I do now?"

"Lorenzo," he yelled, "you mean you never did a play?"

"No," I answered. "I've always been afraid I'd fall off the stage."

I was going to do the play, but the studio wouldn't cut me loose to do it. It would have been a mistake anyway, because it was during my fourth or fifth year of *Magnum*, and I could've lost a lot of money.

I met Kenny Rogers in the early 1970s when I lived in a small apartment on Gorham Street in Brentwood, not too far from where O. J. Simpson lived when Nicole was murdered. Kenny hadn't quite made it big yet. In fact, he was driving a rusted-out Lincoln Continental that ran like hell. One day he had to go to Las Vegas for a gig. It was a long haul from L.A., so he called me the night before and asked if we could switch cars for a week.

His Lincoln was equipped with a car phone, something I'd never seen before, so naturally I agreed.

He gave me the car phone number, told me I could use it if I needed to, took my Jaguar, and split. The next day, four old friends from Chicago showed up at my front door, broke and in need of a way to get to San Diego. One guy's father was sick—or so he said—so I agreed to lend them the Lincoln.

I should have known better.

Kenny came back the next week and dropped off my new Jaguar with a cigarette burn on the seat. I told Kenny that he had to pay to repair it. He did—but then a couple of weeks later, he called me up, very upset.

"Your turn," he said. "I just got my car phone bill and you owe me $262.50."

My Chicago buddies were gamblers. It turned out they called every damn bookie joint and racetrack guy in the area betting horses. I didn't have much cash at the time, so I avoided Kenny for awhile. Fifteen years later, Selleck and I went to see Kenny in concert at the Blazedale Center in Honolulu.

"Ladies and gentlemen," Kenny greeted the audience, "I want to introduce Mr. Tom Selleck from *Magnum, P.I.*"

The place seated 3,500 people. Every one of them was roaring for Tom.

"I also want to introduce Larry Manetti, whom I've known for years and who plays Rick on the show. Stand up, Larry!" I stood up and the crowd applauded just as loudly as they had for Tom. It was pretty nice.

"While he's up," Kenny continued, "I want you all to know that fifteen years ago Larry owed me $262.50, but he stiffed me. Since then, he's tried to pay me back many times, but I never accepted it because he didn't pay it when he should have. I want to hold it over his head so all of you know never to lend Larry Manetti money."

The audience roared with laughter. It was funny, I guess, but still pretty humiliating.

Once Selleck and I were at LaGuardia airport waiting for a flight. We were seated in the Green Room, a room reserved for special travelers. An employee told us, "You gentlemen are going to be in the company of a very special lady." A moment later, Bette Davis was escorted into the room.

I turned to Tom and said, "Fasten your seatbelts, it's going to be a bumpy ride!"

It was a year or two before Bette's death. She looked fragile and was still smoking. She held a long cigarette holder and her manner was very regal. She turned to me and said imperiously, "Young man, light my cigarette." I nervously obliged.

Then she turned to Selleck and said, "You are as handsome as they say. You could be a double for Clark Gable." She should know; she worked with him.

She barely took notice of me. If I hadn't lit her cigarette, she probably wouldn't have known I was there.

〰

Robert Wagner and Natalie Wood, God bless her soul, were in Hawaii in 1980 when we first started *Magnum*. Nancy and I were having dinner in Michele's Restaurant when the Wagners walked in. Robert came over to our table to congratulate me on the series and bought us a bottle of champagne. It was really a big thrill for me at that time. After dinner, I sent him a cordial and he invited us over. We stayed until closing time, but before we left, Natalie Wood decided that she wanted a hot fudge sundae. I begged and bribed the hostess, who was the only employee left in the restaurant, to let me into the kitchen. She helped me unlock the freezer and get the ice cream. Then I found the fudge, nuts, and cherries and made Natalie's dessert. That was the last time I ever saw Natalie Wood. She died in 1981.

Two years later, Nancy and I were in an L.A. restaurant and spied Robert Wagner with some friends. At that time, I was carrying twenty-five dollars in cash and a credit card that was almost maxed out.

"Send drinks over to Robert Wagner and whoever he's with," I instructed the waiter.

"Okay," he said. "Are you sure?"

"Absolutely. Whatever they're having, give them another one."

Well, hell, I didn't know Wagner drank Lafitte-Rothschild wine. The waiter delivered two bottles to their table, and when I got the bill I couldn't pay it. I had to leave my driver's license and a wristwatch in the restaurant to guarantee that I'd be back to pay the bill.

The next day, I went all over town borrowing money to pay the wine bill. To this day, I'm sure Robert Wagner doesn't even know what happened. Every time I think of Lafitte-Rothschild, I think of him.

Tony Curtis is a great movie star whose career was at its height in the fifties and sixties. I first met him in 1973 while visiting the set of the movie *Lepke*, a story about a Mafia mobster in the 1930s. Shortly after, when I was doing *Baa Baa Black Sheep*, Tony's daughter, Jamie Lee Curtis, got a recurring role as a nurse on the show. We became very friendly, and she dated my friend W. K. Stratton for a long time. She is a really good person.

In the mid-'80s Curtis came over to Hawaii to change his lifestyle. We spent a lot of time together. He is a great artist and during that time he would do a painting each day; he was like a factory. I would watch, thoroughly impressed, as he drew pictures while telling stories of the old days in Hollywood. One time Selleck and I had dinner with Curtis. While we were sitting in the restaurant, Tony sketched a picture of Tom, a picture of me, and one of Tom and me together. For some reason, he also drew a picture of a cat, but I have no clue why. Several years later he visited my home in California and noticed the drawings that he had done.

"Larry," he said, "do you know that each of those pictures is worth at least $5,000 today?"

"Really?" I asked. "How about doing another one then?"

"No way," he laughed.

My good friend Freddie Piluso owns Scruples Bar, a very happening spot on Waikiki Beach. Freddie was always friendly with Lee Majors, who is a fun kind of guy. One time, while we were shooting *Magnum*, Lee was in Hawaii. He was supposed to meet Freddie and me at Scruples.

Freddie is never late for anything, but for some reason, on this evening, he was running behind. I was also running a little bit late, and Majors, who's never on time, showed up five minutes early.

Majors waited for about twenty minutes. He could not believe that Freddie was late. While he waited, he strolled over to the doorman and offered to work the entrance greeting the customers. That evening, for a period of time, every customer who entered Scruples was greeted by Lee Majors, and they were ecstatic. Here was the Six Million Dollar Man, the star of *The Fall Guy* series, and he was glad-handing everyone. By the door was a cash register for patrons to pay a cover charge. Instead, Lee gave each patron who walked in the door five dollars from the cash register. Freddie finally showed up forty-five minutes late, and Lee had already handed out over fifteen hundred dollars.

I bet Freddie never kept Lee waiting again.

Chapter 7

The Cast, Producers, and Directors

he costars of *Magnum* truly loved each other. When a cast gets along the way we did, it's a primary reason for the staying power of a TV show. Viewers can see it and feel it, too. Many times when we were doing a scene, I could have taken the pages of the script and thrown them away because the scene would still have flowed. When I looked at the other actors, I knew what they were going to say.

If a new director was doing the show, he might say, "I don't like this." We'd say, "Well, too bad. We do, and we know what we're doing." It was our formula, and we knew exactly what worked. We weren't out of line, but Tom was the boss, and if Tom said it was funny, it was funny.

Magnum, P.I. really came together during the third season. It became so easy. For us, going to work was like brushing our teeth in the morning. It just seemed natural.

I know the camaraderie of the four costars helped the show become a hit. Again, that camaraderie was sincere because offstage we were the same. I don't think there has been any other hit show where two actors shared the same motor home, like Roger Mosley and I, and had a guy like Selleck come banging on the door, saying, "Come on, let's go out." And we'd go out and just have a ball.

Magnum was Roger Mosley's first series. The only other major black television star before Roger was Bill Cosby, and that was when he did *I Spy*. Roger had been in movies such as *The New Centurions, The Greatest, Semitough,* and *Lead Belly,* and was also in TV movies and miniseries such as *Roots, The Jericho Mile,* and *Attica.* He joined *Magnum* because he had a gut feeling that Tom Selleck was a winner even though Tom had made several pilots that didn't sell. Plus, it was so damned cold in Ohio where he had just finished filming *Attica* that he couldn't wait to go someplace warm.

Roger told me about his pre-acting days when he vacuumed cars in a car wash and shined shoes. After work, he would go across the street to the drug store and read every comic book. Roger felt that reading comics helped him to get ideas about how to play fantasy characters.

Mosley was a basketball freak. He played often and was very good. Also an excellent boxer, Roger once sparred with Larry Holmes when Holmes was the heavyweight boxing champion.

Roger took lessons so he could learn to fly a helicopter like his character, T. C. I would never fly with him since I was scared to death of flying anyhow. He became very proficient at handling the choppers, but the insurance company still wouldn't let Roger fly during the TV series.

We were very close friends. When filming, we lived in what they call "honey wagons," which are huge trailers with four cubicles in which actors can rest or sleep. Then Tom bought Roger and me a brand-new, forty-foot motor home as a gift. Roger didn't smoke, but I did, and he hated it. We were like *The Odd Couple*. I had my own phone installed in the motor home, and he'd get a big kick out of answering it and screwing around with the callers. We really had a good time.

The camaraderie between the cast members was no act: We are truly friends.

But at night, he'd go his way and I'd go mine, and we had our own places when we weren't working.

Roger entertained big-name football players who'd visit Hawaii. I'd invite friends from my old neighborhood, tough guys. They would all come to our dressing room, and it was a very wild combination.

Roger Mosley wrote one episode of *Magnum, P.I.* and directed another. He really enjoyed both experiences, and I think he's anxious to do more writing and directing. He's always involved in community projects in L.A. and spends a lot of time at the Watts Repertory, an acting company he established in his old neighborhood. Roger also owned a hair salon and a nightclub in Honolulu.

John Hillerman had a different lifestyle than me. He preferred caviar and champagne. He was like his character, right on the dime. He was wonderful, warm, and very proper, a true gentleman. Some of the directors even called him the Lord.

I used to terrorize John. I think the last thing that John wanted to do was hang out with me off the set. In fact, a couple of times when he entered a restaurant and found out that I was there, he briskly walked out. It wasn't that he disliked me, I just made him crazy. If I knew I could get to him, I would. I'd put crazy glue on a string and stick it on top of his hair when he was sitting in a chair, then watch his toupee fly off when he moved. Another time I nailed his shoes to the floor.

Hillerman was an electronics freak. He was the first guy I knew who had a big-screen TV and gadgets in his house like those from the James Bond movies. For example, the drapes in the windows were electronically operated. He was also the first guy I ever saw with a cellular phone.

John is very intelligent and used fancy words that I needed a dictionary for. A very conservative dresser, he carried a small, battery-operated electronic fan with him in case he became too warm while outside. He also walked with a cane that converted into a portable chair should he desire to sit. And John was never without his Big Red chewing gum.

Hillerman considered himself a poker aficionado and often played with me and Selleck. But what he loved more than anything was playing Trivial Pursuit. He considered himself the best there was at that game. However, he and Selleck came out pretty even in head-to-head competitions.

John loves all the good things in life: caviar, chauffeurs, gardeners, housekeepers, and so on. He bought a penthouse worth over a million dollars in Honolulu. He had a great library in the house; he is a very serious reader and was always buying books for his collection. He's come a long way. I remember him telling us stories about when he couldn't afford the thirty dollars a month rent for a dump in New York.

Interestingly, Hillerman is not British, nor did he go to the finer schools in the East. He was born and raised in Texas. But when he was in the Air Force, somebody took him to a community theater in Fort Worth, Texas. As a result, he decided he wanted a career on the stage. He took a year of intensive voice training in New York, which changed the way he spoke.

Hillerman loved playing Higgins, the British majordomo. He felt it was one of the better parts in TV and he could have done it forever without getting bored. John enjoyed playing people who were smart and who could turn a really good insult.

I consider John Hillerman an outstanding actor. He played the redneck sheriff in the movie *Paper Moon*, had a part in the movie *Lucky Lady*, was on the *Ellery Queen* series for a long time, and played the ex-husband in *The Betty White Show*. He resumed his old Texas twang for his costarring role in the movie *Blazing Saddles*.

107

We were proud and elated when John Hillerman won an Emmy for Best Supporting Actor in a Dramatic Series in 1987. He had been nominated four years in a row, 1983 to 1986. John insisted it wasn't a big thing. But true to John's persona, he acknowledged that he got the award for a body of work on *Magnum*, and he gave a lot of credit to the other actors.

Tom had tried to convince John to attend the awards show that year because he was certain that John was going to win. But Hillerman chose to stay in Hawaii. He was filming a public service announcement for the Houston Symphony at Magic Island.

Tom announced to the audience, "I told the little fart to come, but he wouldn't do it."

The next day, John acknowledged that Tom had encouraged him to attend. Instead, he celebrated alone in his Waikiki apartment with some beluga caviar and champagne.

John was approached quite often from numerous production companies to do other TV series, including a spinoff of his *Magnum* character, Higgins.

〜〜〜

Elisha Cook Jr. was a wonderful actor, too—the last of the great character actors. He had done four or five movies with Humphrey Bogart. Cook was a recurring character in *Magnum, P.I.*, acting in probably fifteen to twenty shows. He played the adoptive father or mentor of my character. He died recently at age ninety-one. Elisha was classy, the most professional guy I ever worked with in my life. Elisha was a great outdoorsman who lived most of the time in a cabin in the woods in Bishop, California, which is in the Sierra Nevadas.

Jeff MacKay played the recurring role of Mac Reynolds. Jeff, who's from Oklahoma, enjoyed making chili, a family specialty. His mom used to visit Hawaii, and we'd have a party in his apartment at the Colony Surf Hotel. She'd make the chili, and Selleck, the cast, and whatever guest stars were in town would come over.

Other recurring cast members were Gillian Dobb (Agatha Chumley), Kwan Hi Lim (Lieutenant Tanaka), Jean Bruce Scott (Maggie Poole), Lance LeGault (Colonel Green), Kathleen Lloyd (Assistant D.A. Carol Baldwin), and Marta DuBois (Magnum's wife from Vietnam). The voice of Robin Masters (used from 1981 to 1985) belonged to Orson Welles.

〜〜〜

An example of the great rapport of the cast and how the episodes mirrored our real-life relationships took place during the episode in which we were marooned on a remote Pacific island. It was formerly a secret base used by the government for testing atomic weapons. T. C., Higgins, Magnum, and my character were on our way to an orphanage for Christmas, and Tom was wearing a Santa Claus costume. The helicopter had engine trouble and we were forced to land on this island. We found out via the radio that the government was going to test a new atomic weapon and the island would be obliterated. They had no idea that we were there, and we all believed we were going to die.

The show revolved around the characters reminiscing about their relationships with each other. My character, Rick, started to come clean with all his goofy stories and stunts in Hawaii that weren't true, or about girls whom he had dated or scored with during the Vietnam War. This heated the group up and they decided that they were going to play a trick. They would scare Rick with insects because they knew he freaks out over them. The guys sent my character, Rick, out to forage for leaves to eat. Higgins, who knew everything about everything, told Rick that there were these leaves that could be eaten, and everyone could live on them if they survived the explosion.

Selleck had rewritten the script and had Rick slipping into a smelly swamp. As I was gingerly climbing out of the swamp, trying not to get my head wet, Tom said, "Here, Rick, let me help you out."

He offered his hand, and as he was pulling me out, I suspected that he was going to do something by the smile on his face. He let go and I fell backwards, headfirst into the swamp. That pissed me off.

In the next scene, Rick was to come out of the bushes, walk to the beach, and tell the guys that he really didn't mind what they had done because they were his good friends. I was kneeling in the bushes out of view as the camera was being set up. On "action," I was supposed to stand up and walk out. Unbeknownst to me, Tom had put a praying mantis on my head. I couldn't feel it because my hair was so wet.

"Okay," the director said, "we gotta get this scene in one shot, Larry. Do you know the lines?"

"Yeah," I answered. "I got it, I got it."

"Let's go. Action!"

*I think John
Hillerman got
a kick out of
seeing me look
like the Swamp
Thing.*

I strolled out and began to deliver my dialogue. I felt something on my forehead, which I figured was a gnat. But then I noticed that this thing had very long legs and I felt a sharp scraping on my forehead. It had dug its claws into my skin to hold on and had maneuvered itself down and over my eyebrows. It was looking into my eye as if to say, *Where the hell am I and who are you?* I couldn't shake it off of my head.

I turned around and screamed, "I'm not afraid of bugs!"

Then I took off running. The cameras were rolling, and I was going, "Ahhhhhhhh!"

I finally got it off my head, but now it was stuck on my hand, and I didn't know if it was going to bite me or what. It wouldn't let go. I'm sure the praying mantis was more frightened than I was, though.

Tom was on *The Merv Griffin Show*, and we surprised him. While he was being introduced by Merv, John Hillerman walked out. About five minutes later, Roger strolled onto the stage. Then I came flying up from the audience screaming. Tom was overwhelmed. He thought we were all on vacation. Merv loved it and enjoyed watching us messing around with each other.

I was sitting next to John when I started throwing the small pillows from the sofa at everyone. John kept muttering under his breath, "Would you please stop it? Behave." I flung a pillow at Griffin and hit him in the head with it. Then I started pushing John's toupee up from the back and it began to slide over his forehead. I could see perspiration beading up on John, but I wanted to have more fun, and I didn't think I had gone too far yet. But I looked at Selleck and he gave me one of those dagger-eyed looks, meaning to knock it off.

Zeus and Apollo were the TV names of the dogs that were used in *Magnum*. They were as integral to the cast as any regulars. When they weren't in a scene, the dogs were kept away from the cast. In the story line, the dogs were never supposed to like any of the costars except for Higgins. They were attack dogs that worked on the estate.

I was very fearful of the Dobermans because they always looked mean. Fortunately, no one was ever bitten. The dogs were usually around in scenes at the estate, and every time they came near me I was afraid. In one episode, Roger and I had to break into the estate, and we were terrified the dogs would tear us to shreds.

The dogs received lots of fan mail, as did the Ferrari and the Robin's Nest estate.

These dog "actors" are called working dogs, like Lassie. They were never seen without their trainer. We were warned never to fraternize with them because these were command-trained dogs; and when the commanders weren't there, you had to fear that they could do something unpredictable.

The first year, local Dobermans (born in Hawaii) were used for half of the season. However, the studio trainer who was working with them left, and the owner of the dogs was brought in to work with them. Problems arose, and the studio had to hire a professional trainer from the mainland.

John Hillerman and Tom insisted that the dogs needed obedience training and not studio training. Scott Hart, a professional trainer, was hired and flown over to finish the second half of the season. The original dogs were two females named Cola and Nohea, and a male called Joe. We always tried to have three or four dogs on hand in case something happened to any of them.

Selleck and Hillerman both got along fine with the "lads" as they were affectionately called by Higgins. The dogs usually stayed near Hillerman, and sometimes with Tom. Hillerman took to the dogs immediately, but it took a little while for them to warm up to him. Tom, however, was a natural with the animals. They loved him right off. I know it impressed Scott Hart that Selleck was great around any type of animal, especially dogs.

Scott decided that he wasn't coming back for the second season, informed Don Bellisario, and returned to the mainland. That summer, Rick Weaver (the son of Dennis Weaver from *Gunsmoke*), an assistant producer on the show, called Scott.

"When you return, we need to know exactly when you're arriving and what type of dogs you're going to use."

Scott told Rick that he wasn't coming back, so Rick immediately sought out Bellisario.

"Do whatever you can," instructed Bellisario, "but get Scott back. And have him get his own dogs and come over early because there is a quarantine period in Hawaii."

Fortunately, Hart agreed, located some Dobermans, and arrived before we began the first episode of the second year. The process of quarantine usually took four months, so we had to get special dispensation from the quarantine office to transport the dogs from the kennel when we needed them to work in the show. During that time, the producer made sure the writers kept any scenarios with the dogs complication free.

After quarantine, the dogs were kept on an old cockfighting ranch near the estate. There was a huge fenced-in yard where they lived until the end of the third year.

At the beginning of the fourth year when we were going into syndication, the production supervisor told Scott Hart that the dogs were being written out of the script. Once syndication begins, studios tend to cut out a lot of complicated stunt work and animals because of the cost.

John and Tom weren't happy about this and went to bat for the dogs. They felt that *Magnum* was getting more dramatic at the time and some comic relief was needed. A decision was made to use the dogs in blocks of time to cut expenses. Thus, for the remaining five years of the series, Scott flew back and forth from California for the four or five episodes in which the dogs were utilized.

A funny story that stands out in my mind about the dogs occurred over a two-day period. Magnum was in Higgins' office using the phone at his desk while the two Dobermans sat at his feet eating small pieces of steak. The cameraman had to shoot the scene showing the dogs eating, then pan over to Tom on the phone with his feet on Higgins' desk. Every time the camera started to pan up, the dogs finished the little pieces of meat so quickly that the trainer had to bring in more and more meat. The scene took a long, long time to shoot, and the dogs ate pounds of steak that day.

The next day there was another scene where John Hillerman met Tom at the front door. Scott Hart was holding the dogs upstairs, and as John talked to Tom, the dogs walked down the steps. Suddenly, everyone started yelling, "Cut!" John and Tom were almost collapsing. It seemed that the dogs had so much gas from eating the steak the day before that they were farting out of control. The crew was hysterical. They had to reshoot the scene over and over again.

Scott Hart brought three dogs over to play Zeus and Apollo. Two were males named Whiskey and Brutus, and the other a female named Dominique. Whiskey, a former junkyard dog that Scott had rescued, never really knew how to play. It took a while to teach him to get along with people because he was used to being a guard dog. He was cautious and always needed to check people out.

The crew always threw what they called mini-wrap parties after each episode. Whiskey would be brought in holding a small beer bucket in his mouth, and the guys would pour him beer and feed him sushi. After a while he became very friendly with everyone. He loved chocolate donuts, even more than he liked steak.

Brutus, a very skinny dog, was found by Scott in Oklahoma. He was intimidated by Whiskey, who Scott had to constantly reprimand for bullying Brutus. Scott finally retrained the Dobermans to walk on opposite sides of him instead of next to each other, which kept Whiskey from brutalizing Brutus.

Scott acquired Dominique, the female, in Pasadena. She was owned by two strange girls who told Scott that Dominique was attack-trained. They put burlap sacks over their heads to demonstrate her aggressiveness, but Dominique never even moved. It took two years for Scott to train Dominique properly. She was smaller than Whiskey and Brutus, but was better at running, leaping, and jumping on people's backs. Dominique was usually in scenes that involved chasing people or performing complicated tricks.

Brutus learned a routine where he lifted his leg on command as if he were peeing. Scott had taught him this for an episode where Higgins had built a huge estate-like dog house. He brought Brutus over and said to the lad, "Why don't you inspect it?" Brutus just lifted his leg.

Brutus hated the water, but Dominique and Whiskey loved it, so they were used in the ocean scenes.

Each dog lived to be about fourteen years old. Brutus died two years ago, and Whiskey died in 1991. They lived long lives for big dogs, but working animals do tend to live longer. I know some animal rights people don't like seeing working animals, but Scott told me that they actually lived longer and better than other dogs because they travel, they're not stressed out, they're not sedentary, they eat well, and they are constantly getting vet checkups. They probably lead the greatest life of any pet.

The dogs received a tremendous amount of international publicity in the fifth year after the show went into syndication in Europe. Lots of international media came to Hawaii to photograph them.

Scott Hart not only trained the lads, but he trained other animals used in the *Magnum* series. He trained a cat that could snarl, and a goat that would ride in the Ferrari. He even trained a macaw to free fly, which is very unusual. We couldn't bring any birds of prey into Hawaii, so we had to use a macaw. Scott also trained the Rottweilers to attack Tom in the two-parter that guest-starred Sharon Stone.

The following producers were involved in *Magnum, P.I.* over its eight-year run. I have listed them in a loose order of impact on the series, but of course, my classification is subjective:

1. Donald P. Bellisario: Co-creator and executive producer for eight years (1980–88).

2. Tom Selleck: Star and also producer of the series during the last couple of years.

3. Charles Floyd Johnson: Producer, supervising producer, co-executive producer, years three to eight (1982–88).

4. Chris Abbott: Producer, supervising producer/writer, years three to eight (1982–88).

5. Reuben Leder: Producer, supervising producer/writer (1981–87). He also directed.

6. Glen Larson: Co-creator of the series; he had very little to do with the series after the pilot episode.

7. Jay Huguley: Writer and later a series producer. Wrote numerous episodes over a three-to-four-year period.

8. Stephen Miller: Producer/writer for one or two years.

9. Jeri Taylor: Producer/writer for one year.

10. Rob Gilmer: Producer/writer for one or two years.

11. Nick Thiel: Producer/writer for one or two years.

12. J. Rickley Dumm: Producer/writer in first two years of the series (1980–82).

13. Rick Weaver: Producer in charge of production in the second year and later in charge of post production.

14. Andrew Schneider: Writer/producer for the first two seasons.

15. Jill Sherman-Donner: Writer/producer for one year.

16. Doug Benton: Supervising producer for one season.

17. Douglas Green: Producer from 1981 to 1982.

18. Joel Rogosin: Producer for one year early on in the series.

There were anywhere from twenty to twenty-five producers over the eight years of the show, but only five had longevity. They included Charles Johnson, Don Bellisario, Chris Abbott,

Charles Floyd Johnson (left) was one of the main producers on Magnum.

Reuben Leder, and, of course, Tom Selleck. Rick Weaver also served as a post-production producer. Chris Abbott was also the story editor, and wrote several *Magnum* episodes.

Charles Floyd Johnson was a producer on *Magnum, P.I.* for six years. He began as a line producer, graduated to supervising producer, and ended up as co-executive producer between 1982 and 1988.

Johnson first met Selleck in 1977 when Tom played Lance White on *The Rockford Files*. He also did the pilot for *Baa Baa Black Sheep* with Stephen J. Cannell, and that was where he met me and Don Bellisario.

Around the third year of *Magnum, P.I.*, the show was in a kind of unsettled period, and Selleck and Bellisario asked Charles Johnson to come over and assist with the production of the show. He arrived in Honolulu for a brief visit and never left.

Later on, Charles joined up with Tom Selleck and Chris Abbott to form Banana Row Productions, and they produced the *B. L. Stryker* series with Burt Reynolds. They stayed together from 1988 to 1993.

Charles went on to do *Quantum Leap* with Bellisario, and eight *Rockford Files* movies-of-the-week. Most recently, he was a co-executive producer on *JAG*.

Born in Middletown, Delaware, Charles attended Stonybrook College Preparatory School in New York. He later received two degrees from Howard University in Washington, D.C.—a Bachelor of Arts degree in political science and a law degree from the School of Law. Voted outstanding senior in law school, Charles was also a member of the *Howard Law Journal* staff, and treasurer of the Student Body Association.

During the late sixties, Charles served in the U.S. Army as a defense counsel. Following that, he returned to Washington, D.C., where he became a member of the Bar and an Attorney Advisor in the U.S. Copyright Office.

Johnson made a big career change when he decided to abandon international law to pursue a career in Hollywood. Jockeying as an actor, writer, and producer, Charles ended up working on *The Rockford Files*, and received his first Emmy award for producing that series in 1978. Next, Johnson produced the pilots for *Simon & Simon* and *Hellinger's Law*. He also produced two public broadcast specials, *Black Filmmakers Hall of Fame* and *Voices of Our People...In Celebration Of*, for which he won two Emmy awards. In addition to the three Emmys he won, Charles has been nominated for seven others.

An active member in many industry and community activities, Charles is currently associated with the Caucus for Producers, Writers, and Directors, and the Academy of Television Arts and Sciences. He's a board member of Media Scope, and treasurer of the Producers Guild of America. He is also a founding member of the Media Forum, which has worked to combat negative media images of minorities.

Additionally, Johnson served as vice president of the board of directors of Communications Bridge, a Los Angeles training program for minority students. Charles has been honored as an outstanding alumnus of both Stonybrook College Preparatory and Howard University, and has also received proclamations from the California and Hawaii State Legislatures.

～～～

Universal hired some of the best directors in Hollywood to do the *Magnum* series, including a number of current and former actors: Jackie Cooper, Ray Danton, Georg Stanford Brown, Stuart Margolin, Ivan Dixon, Robert Loggia, and David Hemmings. The show tried to employ a stable group of directors so they would be familiar with the characters and plot lines. They knew the "bible" of the show. Ivan Dixon, Michael Vejar, Russ Mayberry, Ray Austin, Larry Doheny, and Alan J. Levi directed about seventy of the episodes. We had a number of feature-film directors who loved the show and just wanted the honor of doing a *Magnum, P.I.* episode. Incidentally, our two-parters were about the equivalent of a feature film.

The directors on our show were like family. Most were freelancers with the exception of Alan J. Levi, who was the only one under contract with Universal Studios. He felt that *Magnum* was the most fun show to work on—being in Hawaii, working fourteen- to sixteen-hour days in balmy, beautiful weather with gorgeous scenery. He couldn't believe that he was actually getting paid for it.

Alan Levi did numerous episodes of *Magnum* during our eight-year run. However, our show is just a small part of his accomplishments in television. He also did the pilots and/or movies-of-the-week for the following series: *Columbo, Knight Rider 2000, B. L. Stryker, The Return of Sam McCloud, The*

We were presenters at the 1982 Emmy Awards ceremony.

Bionic Challenge, The Six Million Dollar Man, The Last Song (Motown), Probe, Voyages, Airwolf, Battlestar Galactica, and *The Incredible Hulk.*

In addition, Alan directed the miniseries *Scruples* and *The Immigrants,* and numerous episodes of *JAG, Dr. Quinn, Medicine Woman, Lois and Clark, The Cosby Mysteries, Robocop, Quantum Leap, Simon & Simon, Airwolf, The Incredible Hulk, The Bionic Woman, The Invisible Man,* and *The Gemini Man.*

Furthermore, Levi has directed over thirty live network specials, the 1968 and 1972 Olympics, and over four hundred national prime-time commercials.

Alan has received two Emmy nominations and awards from the Cannes International Film Festival, the International Television and Film Festival of New York, the International Broadcasting Association, the Hollywood Television Society, the American Television and Radio Festival, and the National Advertising Council.

I first met Alan J. Levi when I was doing *Baa Baa Black Sheep*. We were just acquaintances, whereas Levi and Bellisario were pretty close friends. When Alan came to Hawaii to work on *Magnum*, he babysat for my son, Lorenzo. It was convenient since he was staying next door to us at the Colony Surf Hotel. He actually suggested the idea, since he felt that Nancy and I weren't getting out and spending enough time alone.

"Look," he'd offer, "I've just got some homework to do. Why don't you two go out and have some fun?"

He must have babysat dozens of times for us, even after we moved to our condo. Often, we'd come home at night and there was Alan, rocking Lorenzo to sleep.

Now that Lorenzo has decided on a film major in college, Alan has become one of his mentors and has taken him under his wing. It's not just because he's a family friend, but when Alan came to Hollywood, he was fortunate to have Dick Powell as a mentor. Dick Powell was not only a popular actor, but also a very good producer and director. He helped Alan with his college education. Alan has always wanted to give something back to younger people, helping out in the same way that Dick helped him.

One of the episodes I remember Alan directing was "The Big Blow." An actress named Sondra Currie was in the show, and Alan and she were very close. When the episode was over, they returned to Los Angeles and moved in together. Today, they are married.

Alan also directed the episode "Smaller than Life," which was a major one for me. He scared me during this show. We were always impressed with John Hillerman, who never memorized a scene until after we had rehearsed and were ready to shoot, and then, of course, he would walk in and pull it off cold. He was tremendous at that, so we all tried to copy him— each of us walking into the rehearsal with the script, figuring we could do it like John.

Alan said to me before we began filming, "You know, Larry, we've got a really good script here, and I know you're gonna be great. But I don't want to catch you walking in with this script in your hand thinking you can pull it off like Hillerman. Because if you don't know the lines, then I'm gonna print whatever we shoot, and you're not going to like it when you see it on television."

Well, he frightened the daylights out of me. I made sure I had it memorized—cold. There were two or three takes and it was over. This was the episode where I worked with Corky the little person, and we had an interesting onscreen relationship. It became one of our most popular shows and generated a tremendous amount of fan mail.

Alan directed the two-part "L.A." episode that starred Dana Delany. We had all seen her on a *Moonlighting* episode, and everyone was very high on her. Alan said, "She's gonna be a star." And, of course, he turned out to be right. She was terrific in *China Beach*.

Probably the best episode that Alan directed was "Death and Taxes." It was nominated for an Emmy award and was a real departure from other *Magnum* episodes. Alan shot it avant-garde-like and used long lenses. It was a complicated shoot, and the audience never really saw the perpetrator or any of the killings.

The *Magnum* producers knew that Alan was taking a big gamble. Before filming, Alan met with Charles Johnson and Tom Selleck.

"Look, I've got an idea for the show, and I'm gonna need a vote of confidence from you guys because you're not gonna like the dailies." Initially they agreed with his idea.

But sure enough, after the second day, Charles Johnson went to Alan very concerned and asked, "What are you doing?" After Alan explained and the subsequent dailies were reviewed, Tom and Charles understood—somewhat.

Alan was editing the episode back in Los Angeles. He decided to pay his own way to fly out to Hawaii to screen "Death and Taxes" with Tom and Charles, because he wanted to explain again what he had done. He also wanted to encourage them to pay $8,000 for music that was not standard for *Magnum, P.I.* episodes. It was original music by a group called Gemini. As it turned out, Charles and Tom loved the show. After that, other directors were given opportunities to use different music and filming techniques, and as a result, produced some really innovative work.

The episode called "Laura" with Frank Sinatra was a wonderful experience for Alan. He'd worked with a lot of different actors over the years, many difficult ones, and he didn't know what to expect with Sinatra.

He flew over to Hawaii early and met with Charles Johnson. "Listen," said Charles, "we're going to have to go up to Frank's penthouse. The room next door to his is laid out with lots of clothes for Frank to choose from for the series, mostly Hawaiian shirts and hats."

Right before they arrived at Sinatra's room, Charles whispered to Alan, "Let Frank pick out the outfits. Don't get involved, or else we're gonna have lots of problems."

So they took Frank into the room with the clothes. There were six Hawaiian shirts displayed on the bed. Frank turned, looked at Alan Levi, and asked, "Which ones do you like?"

Charles Johnson whispered to himself, "Oh my God."

"I like this shirt for the majority of the episode," said Alan, "and for the last two scenes, this one."

"Hey, that's great!" exclaimed Frank. "These are just the ones I would have picked out . . . So, kid, where are the hats?"

"Kid" was Frank's term of endearment. They walked over to where the hats were. Charles Johnson was a wreck at this point.

Sinatra turned to Alan. "Well, kid, which hats do you like?"

Alan chose different hats, similar to the ones that Frank wore when he was a young crooner in New York and drove the bobbysoxers wild. Frank loved the hats, and at that, he grabbed Alan and said, "What do you drink, kid? Let's go out and have a belt." From that point on they got along great.

An interesting incident during the "Laura" episode took place on a rooftop where Frank's character finally caught the guy who killed his granddaughter. In the scene, Sinatra's character is fighting the murderer, who accidentally falls off a seven-story building and is killed. We knew that Frank had to go back to the states for an operation, and Alan did not want Frank doing dangerous stunts on the edge of the rooftop of a tall building.

So we were all sitting in our director's chairs: me, Tom, Alan, and Sinatra. Frank leaned over to Alan and whispered, "You're gonna let me do this fight sequence, right?"

"Gee, Frank," answered Alan, "I'm kinda worried. Let's forget it."

"No," insisted Frank, "I want to do it."

"All right, Frank, but just the closeups, okay? For the long shots, we've got to have a stunt man because it's too close to the edge of the rooftop."

Frank agreed, and then a couple of minutes later he came back to Alan and said, "If you ever tell my doctor that I really did this scene, kid, I'm gonna kill ya."

Sinatra was the type of actor who preferred one take only, and anytime Alan had to repeat a scene, he would very quietly go over and explain to Frank that by reshooting the scene it would really emphasize the moment. As long as Alan said this to Frank, alone, out of earshot of anyone else, everything was okay.

We were supposed to shoot a scene at a banquet hall where Frank's character is retiring. He was in front of all of these police officers, and it was a very long shot beginning on a line of seated cops and then moving to Frank, who would walk to the podium. Alan had rehearsed this scene with the camera operator a few times, emphasizing that it had to be good and that it could only be shot once.

Alan called, "action," and halfway through the sequence, the cameraman slipped off of the dolly. Frank looked up, stepped back, and called out to Alan, "Who do you have operating the camera? Stevie Wonder?"

Well, we thought that was it for the day, but the assistant cameraman suddenly screamed out, "Mr. Sinatra!" He pulled out ten feet of film from the camera and said that there was a mechanical jam. Frank said, "Okay, let's do it again." Actually, there was no jam. The assistant was just covering up for the cameraman who had slipped. After the scene, Frank walked over to Alan and asked, "Did we really have a jam?"

"I guess we'll never know, will we, Frank?"

The last day of shooting the "Laura" episode, Sinatra had to leave the set at three-fifteen to get on a plane to fly back to the states for the operation. He walked in and told Alan, "Kid, I'm leaving at three-fifteen. I know you'll never finish me by three-fifteen, but it's gotta happen."

Alan said, "It'll happen."

"It'll never happen," responded Frank.

"I hear you're a betting man," said Alan. "We'll see, won't we?"

At the end of the scene, Frank put his arms around Alan, whispered something in his ear, and walked out. It was five after three.

Chapter 8

Working in Paradise

e were blessed to have filmed *Magnum, P.I.* in one of the most scenic areas in the world—the Hawaiian Islands. Although they are too numerous to list, I've included some of the more popular sets and locations from the show:

Robin's Nest was actually the idyllic Eve Anderson Estate located thirty miles outside of Honolulu. It had a large turtle pond, a Hawaiian-style, open-air home, and many birds and birdcages. The beach was tranquil, and I loved to paddle around in the salt water when I wasn't working. Interestingly, the set for the guest house was located on a sound stage at Diamond Head Studio that had originally been used for *Hawaii Five-O*. It wasn't soundproof, and we had to stop shooting scenes frequently when a noisy truck drove by.

We used several locations for my character Rick's club, the King Kamehameha Club, beginning with the Elks Club in Honolulu. Then we moved to a state park on the beach where we built a set. Later, we relocated to the Kahala Hilton Hotel, but we couldn't control the noise level due to the crowds of tourists. So finally, we went back to the state park. The interiors were beautifully adorned; everything was topnotch due to my character requiring the best clothes, shoes, office, and so on. Fans actually believed I owned a real King Kamehameha Club. And later, of course, Tom and I opened the Black Orchid Restaurant.

T. C.'s charter helicopter business, the Island Hoppers, was first located near the Ala Wai Yacht Harbor and later on the Makai Research Pier. Incidentally, T. C.'s office was always neat because Roger insisted his character maintain a clean living image. Roger was rarely, if ever, seen drinking or smoking. Basically, he was the opposite of my character. Roger loved kids, too, and was a great role model for them.

Little Saigon was situated on Hotel Street in Honolulu. This area served as the location for various settings in Hawaii and the Far East. Being a very historic district, it could double for a Chinatown in Hawaii or San Francisco, or a place in Vietnam.

We shot many scenes at the University of Hawaii located in Manoa Valley, which was quite beautiful. I can't imagine a prettier campus. Often, I'd go there just to escape and read.

The Pali Tunnels were man-made, bored through volcanic mountains. We shot a lot of drive-through scenes there. As a result of the show, the Valley of the Temples became a popular tourist stop. The Valley and other places had never been filmed for a TV series before. Instead of emphasizing only the beach, *Magnum* filmed cultural areas, and they became part of the tours to the islands as well.

Most of the people who worked on *Magnum, P. I.* as extras were local Hawaiians. Locals also played all the Hawaiian music and catered our meals. The food was very healthy. It became a big part of my life. I remember times when they'd catch an octopus and cut it up right on the pier. The caterers would insist, "Get over here. Have some." Who would think a kid from Chicago, from a ghetto in an Italian neighborhood, would ever observe an octopus being taken straight out of the

In addition to the dogs on the show, we also used a macaw. Why do I always seem to get stuck with the animals?

129

ocean, cut up, and eaten on the spot? The Hawaiians had a very friendly way about them, which made me feel at home. They'd say, "Here, try this." And I'd say, "Aghhhhh," but I'd try it anyway out of respect. And I was always surprised that everything I tried, I liked.

I got friendly with Joe Bordonaro, the owner of a string of Japanese sushi restaurants. One day he called in a panic. All of his sushi chefs from Japan were locked up at Immigration and Naturalization because of a problem with their citizenship papers. Without the chefs, the business would have to close down. So I made a cold telephone call to an administrator in the office of the Director of Immigration. Luckily, the guy turned out to be a friend of mine whom I had known since I arrived in Hawaii.

"I'll release the guys," he said, "but the favor that I want in return is that when I come by tonight, I want to see you in a Japanese outfit serving me and my wife sushi."

This was a tough favor since, at the time, I hated the smell of raw fish. But I acquiesced. They came for dinner, took some photos, and even made me taste a California roll.

I can understand why people who live in or even visit Hawaii never want to leave. The culture is incredible. Many people think Hawaii's very commercial, but it's not. Hawaiians believe that it's a bad omen if you take a shark out of the water and kill it. Even the volcanic rock is not supposed to be taken off of the island. Tourists take it and use it for barbecues or souvenirs, but the Hawaiians don't approve of that.

There are different islands in Hawaii, each with its own set of characteristics. There's an island where probably the best chocolate in the world is made, and a lot of people don't know this. The macadamia nuts and the Kona coffee grown on the islands are awesome, too. Hawaii's the only state in the country that grows coffee. There is snow skiing and beautiful pine trees on the big island.

If you look at weather patterns like the ones shown on the news, you'll see that the jet streams miss Hawaii. The jet streams produce bad weather across Canada and the northern United States. In the Southern Hemisphere, it goes the other way. There, right in between all the bad weather, in the perfect location, is Hawaii. Sure, there's an occasional hurricane or typhoon, but that's an easy price to pay for living in paradise. Compare the newspaper headlines in any major city in the United States to Honolulu, and I'll bet you'll find that there is more violence in one day than in ten years in Honolulu. People don't lock their doors in Hawaii. I think the biggest thing that ever happened while I lived there was when an elephant went berserk, escaped, and had to be killed. He had killed his trainer and gone on a rampage through the streets of Honolulu.

I came to appreciate the lifestyle in Hawaii as I grew accustomed to the culture, people, and environment. I went through a transitional period when I first arrived. I had a very hot temper, and although I was frustrated, I was able to learn how to calm myself down while living there. I learned how to relax with saunas, gentle exercise, and working with light weights. I also enjoyed taking long walks on the beach wearing ankle weights, and vitamins became a part of my daily routine.

By the time the show was over, I loved Hawaii and its healthy lifestyle, which is much slower paced than on the mainland, especially the metropolitan areas where I came from. It's as close to God as I'm ever going to get—truly paradise. Every day is beautiful. The sky is blue, there are stars in the sky every night, and the air is fresh and clean. It took me a few years to get used to not being there after *Magnum* ended.

My worst nightmare came to life during the years I spent in paradise: fins gliding through the water, attached to a twenty-five-foot body and a mouth full of sharp, pointy teeth.

Sharks were everywhere in the waters around Hawaii—one good reason I had become deathly afraid of the ocean. But from time to time, the script would call for me to dive into the ocean. And whenever it did, I panicked.

I remember an episode in which Tom had been lost at sea for a couple of days and everybody was looking for him. I was searching for him by boat, T. C. and Higgins by helicopter. When we found him, it was my job to dive into the water to rescue him.

The crew had designated an area that I was supposed to jump into. When the moment came, I took some deep breaths and reminded myself that divers were protecting the whole area with bang sticks. If a shark came around, the divers could use them to stun or even kill it.

Wouldn't you know that just as I was leaping heroically off the boat, I heard someone yell, "Shark! Shut it down! Shark in the water!"

Too late! I was already in. Just in time to see this great big shadow that must have been twenty-five feet long approaching me. All I can say is that my legs must have moved like a Saturday morning cartoon character's, a hundred miles an hour through the water. I jumped onto Tom's shoulders, holding on for dear life, nearly drowning both of us in my panic. After the shark departed, we shot the scene over and over. It took forever to get it right and I was nervous the whole time.

As a result of *Magnum, P.I.*, I made many, many personal appearances in numerous places. I took trains and planes, drove trucks and vans, went all over the world. Not only for the money, but for also for charity, visiting scores of hospitals and entertaining children.

Personal appearances are extra perks, which many actors never consider when they enter the profession; and only recognition from a continuing TV series or blockbuster movie can provide it. I did bar mitzvahs, weddings, and birthday parties. I even flew to Detroit, Michigan once and popped out of a cake for a little girl who was a big fan of *Magnum, P.I.* I made anywhere from $5,000 to $25,000 for a personal appearance. Citibank once paid me $10,000 for a day's work.

I had some crazy offers, too: women who wanted to buy clothes from Selleck; a guy who said that if I got the Ferrari from the show, he would pay me triple what it was worth; a woman who offered me a hundred grand, and even put it in her will to see to it that when she died she'd be buried in Tom Selleck's Ferrari.

Many manufacturers offered Tom and the rest of us big bucks to merchandise the show, but we were all opposed to the idea. We didn't want *Magnum* dolls and cars to saturate the toy stores because we felt it would cheapen the show. I hope everybody understands that, because a lot of series put out numerous products to try to get everything they can out of their show before it goes off the air. In our case, we wanted to put everything into the series, hoping that we could keep it a quality show for as long as it was on the air.

I was in love with the fire-engine-red Ferrari that we used in the *Magnum* series. Although it was out of my financial reach, I decided I had to have one. In 1984, the studio replaced the original Ferrari with a newer one, and I bought the old one. Since the car was used as a "tow car" on the series—meaning that it was really being towed when Tom appeared to be driving it on the screen—it had hardly any miles on it when I bought it. I thought I was getting a great deal.

But actually, the car was in pretty bad shape. The paint had deteriorated from being in the hot sun all the time, and it probably never had a tune-up or an oil change because it was never really driven on the show. I had shipped the Ferrari to L.A. during our hiatus period, and I learned the hard way that it should not have been driven in bumper-to-bumper traffic.

It was seven o'clock on a very hot Friday evening in August, and I was on the Ventura Freeway. All of a sudden, the car died. There were hundreds of cars on the freeway blowing their horns. I climbed out of the car and tried to get across the freeway. As I was standing there, some guy pulled up and yelled, "Hey, Rick, why don't you call Magnum and get a tow?"

Two minuses of doing a show in Hawaii were the distance from the continental U.S. and the importance of my role to an eight-day episode cycle. Once, while I was involved in a three-episode cycle that shot for one month, my brother called to tell me his firstborn son had died of sudden infant death syndrome. I wasn't able to get on a plane and go comfort him because I was the cover set. When it rained, everyone had to run for cover under the roof. In the tropics, the weather was very unpredictable. Only God knew when it would rain. My scenes were always underroof, so they'd tell me to stay put, and if it rained, they'd film me inside. Anyhow, I was forced to live with the guilt of not being there for my brother.

Shortly after that, my dad called with the news that my mother had suffered a stroke and was on life-support equipment. Again, the studio could not permit me to leave because of the shooting schedule. But this time it was too much. I told them I was out of there, and they could shove it if they didn't like it.

When I was a kid, my mother often gave me elephant statues and keepsakes because she believed that they brought good luck. I kept all of them, and by the time *Magnum* went on the air, I must have had a collection of fifty or sixty different elephants. They were made from every material imaginable except for ivory, because an elephant would have to be killed to acquire the ivory. Somehow, one of the national magazines got wind of my elephant collection and asked me if they could take a picture of it. After the article appeared, I began receiving elephant gifts from people all over the world.

My son loved them too, so on one of his birthdays I had an animal trainer bring over a real elephant named Tigh. The elephant was standing calmly on my front lawn while my son fed it peanuts and apples. Suddenly it began to backup frantically. Tigh backed his ass right through my picture window in the front of the house. He continued into the living room, stopping only after he had wrecked a quarter of our home.

〰〰

Over eight years of filming, some pretty interesting and amusing things happened. The Kaiser Hospital in Honolulu was going to be demolished, so we synchronized the explosion of the building with one of our episodes. According to the script, I was supposed to run from the building covered with dust and soot. However, I became disoriented, and, instead of running toward the camera, I ran out the wrong way. When I realized it, I reentered the hospital, ran back through the demolished area, and finally found the correct way out. In the meantime, I forgot my lines and panicked. Everyone was staring at me, waiting for my lines, since we all knew that we couldn't shoot another take because the building had already been blown up. So, I ad-libbed and said something like, "What I need is a good Chinese laundry."

We shot an episode where I was convicted of murder and sent to a brand-new prison. I was actually the first inmate to be incarcerated at Halawa Prison. Since all of the scenes were shot in my cell and the surrounding area, instead of walking to my motor home between shots, I got a blanket and slept in the cell. It became my home for ten days.

I also wrote a message on the cell wall: "Larry Manetti slept here." It was fun for a few days, but then it got scary. I still remember the clanging sound of the gates when the doors opened and slammed shut. I thought, *There ain't no way I'm ever going to get out.* Considering all my brushes with the law, it hit a little too close to home.

～～～

There were a few incidents involving crackpots who flew to Hawaii and became big problems. The Hawaiian police were very good; they would catch these stalkers and crackpots, and put them on a plane out the next hour. The protection was unbelievable. I knew about stalkers early on because a child molester had pursued me when I was a preteen.

When I agreed to become the spokesman for the Exchange Club for abused kids, it was the first time in probably over two decades that I had talked about the time I was almost kidnapped by a child molester. It was something that I had kept inside until then. Actually, I've never forgotten the pervert's face.

I was twelve when my dad sent me to visit relatives in the town where he was raised in Michigan. The family packed my clothes and put me on a train. There was a man in his mid-thirties who had asked to be put in the berth above mine. He obviously knew how to pick his mark. He talked to me a lot, and bought my food, and I thought it was cool. Then he suggested that we go for a little walk, and he walked me into a vacant car on the train. I didn't know what he had in mind, but luckily, a conductor appeared and said that we weren't allowed there, and had to return to our berth. At one point during that night, he tossed me down a copy of something pornographic, but I was too tired to be interested in it.

I arrived in Michigan safely and everything was fine. When I was returning at the end of the week, the guy was on the train again. He talked to me and offered me a cigarette, which was, of course, a big deal for a kid my age.

About a week after I got home, I came out of school, and the same guy from the train was sitting there in a truck. He had been stalking me. Later, he was waiting in front of my house when I got home. My grandma was there, and he approached the door and asked for me. She told him I couldn't come out. He had been there earlier and asked her when I would be home. Grandma figured something was wrong and called my dad. He sensed trouble right away, so he called the cops and gave them a description of the guy's truck.

When I left school the next day, the guy was there again, and the cops nabbed him. They couldn't hold him because he didn't do anything to me, even though they discovered that he had a record and had been to prison for molesting children. I remember my dad sitting me down and telling me about what happened and saying that I had to be very careful. I was lucky, but many kids aren't. I'm still involved with the Exchange Club

Foundation for the Prevention of Child Abuse. I hope that my involvement can help spare other kids from a horrible experience like mine.

~~~

Occasionally, we had problems with overzealous fans of the show. There was the time an intruder climbed onto Tom's rooftop. Tom awoke to the sound of footsteps on his roof and knew right away they didn't belong to an animal. The next thing he knew, the lights went out. The intruder had cut the power lines, but fortunately, not the phone lines, so Tom was able to call the police. Within a few minutes they surrounded the house, scaled the roof, grabbed the stalker, and hauled him off to jail.

It turned out the guy was a religious fanatic who had tried and failed to get Tom before. He was released from jail the next day—Tom declined to press charges—then banned from the island and put on an airplane. The media never heard about this incident or about any of the other crazies who stalked the cast from time to time. We were afraid news like this would only encourage copycat incidents.

Not that we weren't protected—local and state enforcement personnel were always guarding the perimeters of the sets, and we had our own private security force. However, none of us wanted personal bodyguards around when we weren't working.

Security-wise we had to be very careful, not only with tourists, but with the extras who were hired to work on *Magnum*. After a somewhat crazy incident, we made a rule that the extras couldn't carry cameras around the set. Here's what happened: Tom was wired up—he had a microphone taped to his chest with a wire running down his pants leg attached to a battery on his ankle. The wire got caught in Tom's shirttail and he had to unzip his fly. As he reached in to adjust his shirt, an extra snapped a picture of him. That was the last straw. We figured that sooner or later that photo would turn up in the *National Enquirer.*

I also had my own special nut encounter. A man flew over to the island with the specific intention of baptizing all the show's stars. I was living by the beach at the time, and the guy somehow found my house and showed up at my door wearing a white sheet. I suppose he was trying to look like Jesus, but the sheet covered his head and had eye-holes, so he looked more like a member of the KKK.

"Come on out, Rick!" he called to me. "It is time for your rebirth. It is time to wash away your sins."

As I walked outside, I whispered to the maid, "Call the cops." Though I was a little freaked out, I tried to humor the guy when he told me he wanted to baptize me right then and there in the ocean.

"Well," I said, "if you want to baptize me, you have to baptize my parrot, too."

I figured that would get rid of him, but it didn't. "So bring the bird," was all he said.

I was trying to figure out a way to stall him until the cops showed up, but as it turned out I didn't have to. As I walked out with my bird the police were already ushering the guy into the paddy wagon.

~~~

One of the scariest incidents took place in Miami when I was making a USA cable network film called *The Take* during a break from *Magnum, P. I.* There was a woman who worked at the hotel where I was staying. She always went out of her way to talk to me. I assumed she was a fan of the show. One day she called my room and invited me to a party. I told her, in a nice way, that I already had plans to meet some friends next door at the cafe.

A few minutes later, I went to the cafe. The guys weren't there yet, so I sat down at the bar. The next thing I knew, this woman, whom I'll call Suzanne, showed up. It was obvious that she had followed me. She started making small talk, and the conversation quickly got strange. She referred to killing somebody in Texas and told me that she'd been in a mental institution and escaped. In an attempt to get away from her, I told her that I had to go to the men's room. She started screaming that she was going to blow my head off. She rose from her seat and threatened everybody in the bar and restaurant. I slid out the back door and hid in the bar of another hotel nearby.

I thought I was safe, but she was still pursuing me. She spotted me in the bar and told me she was going to kill me. Suzanne had a big purse, and I was afraid she had a gun in it. I ran out of the hotel, through a parking garage, into the hotel where I was staying, and onto the elevator. Again, I thought I had escaped. But the elevator stopped, the door opened, and she rushed in. The elevator door closed, and we were alone. As I suspected, she had a gun and it was pointed right at my belly. I figured I was history, but I guess my survival instincts took over. I quickly grabbed her wrist and pushed the gun away from me. We struggled until I was able to push her off balance and she fell. When the elevator doors opened, I ran out. She was still screaming that she was going to blow me away.

I ended up fleeing the hotel, hailing a taxi, and going over to the apartment of one of the producers who lived nearby. I filed a report with the hotel security and police, and the studio provided me with around-the-clock security. Eventually, Suzanne's car was found in a parking lot, but they couldn't find her. Somehow she managed to locate me, though, and called my room threatening to find me and kill me no matter how long it took. The police never did locate her, and it really shook me up for awhile.

∽∽

I was in Hawaii nine months each season beginning in approximately June and ending around February. We could leave, but we had to have permission, especially me. As I mentioned earlier, I was always on a chain because I was part of the cover set, and my scenes were mostly inside. We were in the tropics where it could rain at any second. My character owned the club, so they wanted me to stick around in case filming had to move indoors. They didn't want me to get in any trouble either, and they were afraid that I might end up in South America.

We went through a lot of producers. They used to come all the time and watch me. That was one of their job responsibilities. This was a multi-million-dollar series, a huge hit. So if I said, "Hey, I think I'm gonna go to New York and get a drink at Sardi's," and they said, "Where is he? We need Manetti," we were in trouble. So babysitting me became part of the producer's responsibility.

We were, however, allowed certain travel courtesies. The costars flew back and forth more frequently because they'd get burned-out doing the show. Selleck got about twenty round trips a year, and I got around six, as did Roger and John.

We all went to London to do one of our two-hour *Magnum* TV movies. The show was about an old friend of Magnum's who was in the service with us in Vietnam. The friend was murdered in London and Tom ended up going over to investigate. Magnum called Rick, and told him that he needed his help.

The producer decided that it would be great if all the stars actually lived in the castle where the show would take place. So the studio rented Leeds Castle, which was originally Henry VIII's home where he was married to all of those women whose heads he chopped off. It was a historical site. Though tours were given every day, nobody had resided in the castle in years.

I wasn't thrilled about it because I had a feeling that the producer had pulled this off to keep me in line or to keep an eye on me. I was always in trouble. I had just moved to my third hotel in London after being kicked out of the first two while we were waiting for filming to commence.

One night I threw all my shoes out the window, and one of them hit the doorman in the head. That got me thrown out of hotel number one.

Then the late Lee Fleischman, a wild and crazy friend from Hawaii, came to stay with me. He met a girl at the hotel bar and went back to her room. After he left her room, he went to the wrong floor and entered what he thought was his own room. The door was ajar, so he entered the room, crawled into bed, and went to sleep. He woke up in the middle of the night, looked around, and decided that he had been robbed. He called the police. The cops arrived just as the couple who actually belonged in the room showed up. They demanded to know what was going on. A great commotion commenced and I went to investigate. That's when everyone realized that Lee was in the wrong room. I got involved, trying to help Lee, and they kicked us out of hotel number two.

So we wound up at Leeds Castle, and Selleck told me that the castle was haunted. I believed him because I'm gullible. My room in the castle had the original stone floors from medieval days. There was this horrid bathroom which had a tank with a chain on the wall for flushing the toilet. You could only use a small amount of toilet paper or the toilet would clog the pipes and the castle would flood.

There were noisy ducks in the moat that honked and kept us up at night. After complaining to the custodian of the castle, I was informed that these big ducks were better security than dogs. They were biting "guard ducks." One day, I found this was true because the ducks chased after me and bit me. Luckily, I had my elevator boots on and they couldn't bite through the heel.

Selleck insisted on having formal dinners every night in the castle. By the third night, I was fed up and wanted to kill

Tom. There was me, John Hillerman, Roger Mosley, Tom, and Charles Johnson, our producer. Charles rang a bell and the dinner staff brought out a nine-course dinner with different wines and liqueurs. I got totally inebriated. Then Tom would say, "Let's retire to the port room." There, the butler served us aged port and cigars, and we'd drink some more.

After the fifth night of formal dining, and not being able to escape this place, I was flipping out. And there was another wonderful treat: no phones except in the manager's office, which was always locked.

Selleck and Johnson kept reminding me that the castle was haunted and they had the manager in on it, too. She said things were often missing, and she had seen a ghost. I was starting to get scared. One night, in the port room, Tom ordered caviar and Cristal champagne. I drank a lot and then I had a nightcap. Suddenly the lights started flickering in the castle.

I asked what it was, and the manager said, "Oh, don't worry. It's probably just a ghost. It happens a lot."

"A ghost!" I yelled.

While the manager kept me busy with ghost tales, a couple of the guys went upstairs to my bedroom, short-sheeted my bed, disconnected my lights, and strung these thin threads across the room. When the door was opened, the wind from the open window blew the white threads making them appear to be floating across the room. They also put brushes at the bottom of my bed under the sheet so that when I stuck my feet under the covers, they would feel like hairy rats.

After the port room closed, I staggered up to my room. When I opened the door to my room, it created a draft from the open window, which blew the threads across the room, making me think I was seeing ghosts.

I screamed, but nobody heard me. They were hiding. I kept screaming, and when nobody responded, I thought, *I must be an idiot. They're going to think I'm crazy.* I slammed the door and got undressed. I had a glass of champagne I had brought to my room, so I sat down in the dark and finished it off. Still holding the glass, I slid under the covers. The short-sheet and brushes met my feet, and I panicked.

"Oh my God!" I gasped, flinging the glass. It hit the stone floor and broke into a million pieces.

The next morning, everyone came to my room to see how I had made it through the night. They saw the broken glass and me shivering in bed. I was shaking not because I was still scared, but because of the broken glass and the "ghosts," I never got out of bed during the night to go to the bathroom. "I have to pee," I confessed as everyone laughed.

Then I looked up and saw the threads and knew I'd been duped. At first I was livid, but then I broke into hysterics, too.

The next night, I decided to slip out of the castle and go to London. There was a service entrance in the rear of the castle where deliveries were made. I told the attendant at the service entrance that I needed to borrow the castle truck because Selleck wanted me to go into town to get this special wine for him. I had never driven in England, and I forgot that you had to drive on the opposite side of the road. I narrowly missed getting into accidents and got lost a dozen times. Miraculously, I arrived in London. I wound up in a pub, not thinking about how I was going to find my way back to the castle. I showed up the next morning just in time for my call. I wasn't soused, because I never drank excessively when I worked, but let's put it this way, I didn't look very rested.

Nancy came over to London towards the end of filming, and John Hillerman invited us to dinner at the posh St. James Club. We met in the bar for cocktails, and Hillerman called our drink order over to the bartender. The guy ignored John, forcing him to walk over to the bar where he berated the guy, who kept his back turned to John.

Finally, after twenty minutes, the drinks arrived, and as I turned around to give the waiter a piece of my mind, I got a great surprise. Dressed as the waiter was my old paparazzi pal from Hawaii, Robin Leach.

He joined us for dinner and rehashed his rise to fame.

Nancy and I hadn't seen Robin since he put us in *Lifestyles of the Rich and Famous* in 1982. He was doing a segment on the most romantic restaurants in the world, and he had the two of us eating dinner at Michele's Restaurant in Oahu. Located right on the beach at the Colony Surf Hotel, the view is unobstructed and breathtaking. And the meal—champagne, caviar, fresh luscious fish—was as good as it gets.

In 1987, I was flown from Hawaii to L.A. to be part of a commentary by four Hollywood actors to discuss the World Middleweight Championship Boxing Match. I was nervous because Jack Palance was one of the actors.

When I first came to L.A. in 1972, I went to a famous place called Barney's Beanery with my friend, Johnny Valentino. There in a corner was Jack Palance eating a bowl of chili. I walked over and introduced myself.

"Mr. Palance, my name is Larry Manetti. I'm from Chicago, Illinois and I'm going to be an actor. I'm a big fan of yours, and I've seen every movie that you ever made."

He didn't look up, but said, "Name them!"

I hurried away with my tail between my legs.

So now it's fifteen years later and I was in Matteo's Restaurant in L.A. Sugar Ray Leonard was fighting Marvin Hagler, and one of the cable networks wanted four actors to give their opinions of the Middleweight Championship. They chose Jack Palance, me, Lainie Kazan, and George Dzundza, who was in the film *Crimson Tide* and was one of the stars of the TV show *Law & Order*.

The commentator began the show. "Ladies and gentlemen, we're here tonight at the famous Matteo's Restaurant where all the stars dine—Frank Sinatra, Dean Martin, Steve and Edie, Milton Berle...Let's see if we can get a few words from the owner, Matty Matteo."

Now, Matty is a very colorful guy who once broke his neck, so his neck is tilted all of the time, and he speaks out of the side of his mouth. Matty sat down between us, all crunched up.

"Matty," asked the commentator, "who do you think is going to win the fight?"

"Well," responded Matty, "the black guy is going to win." Leonard and Hagler, of course, were both black.

The commentator regrouped and said, "Matty, with all the customers in here, the food must be excellent. What's your most popular dish?"

"The dish I like is the fusilli," said Matty. "You get the fusilli with the marinara sauce and you pour this red pepper on it, and it will burn your whole asshole out!"

Jack Palance and I slithered underneath the table. I never did remind Jack Palance about our first meeting. I still couldn't name all of his movies.

145

〰️

In the final episode of *Magnum*, we used some of our friends from the restaurant business. Nicky Blair, who owns a restaurant named after him in Los Angeles, appeared in our last show along with Randy Schoch, the co-owner of Nick's Fish Market in Hawaii.

This finale, entitled "Resolutions," was our last *Magnum* after eight years, 162 hours of programming, and about $200,000,000 in total production spending.

"Resolutions" took twelve days to complete. On the last day, there was very tight security, lots of emotion, and some paranoia on the part of a couple staff members. We had over a dozen guards maintaining crowd control, and tourists actually held a vigil along the highway hoping to catch a glimpse of Selleck.

We went overboard trying to keep the plot of the last episode a secret. There were hundreds of freelance journalists and photographers following us everywhere trying to get a crew member to leak the plot.

The Eve Anderson Estate, which was the fictional home of Robin's Nest, served as a fitting place for us to end the series. I'm sure the Andersons miss the money, but I know they don't miss the mess or damage. The production company probably caused some of it, but the tourists who tried to break in by climbing over the gate because so many of them believed Selleck actually lived there also share some of the blame. I don't know how much Ms. Anderson made from the years we used her home, but there was gossip that it exceeded $1,000 a day.

I also heard that by the time we were finished shooting *Magnum*, Universal figured out that it cost $400,000 more per episode to shoot the show in Hawaii than in Los Angeles.

Chapter 9

Trouble with the Law

I was in a 1974 movie that was being filmed in Maryville, California called *Melvin Purvis, G-Man*, starring Dale Robertson. I played the best friend of the notorious gangster, John Dillinger. Dan Curtis, a pretty famous director, was directing the movie.

One evening, I was eating in the hotel dining room with Dale Robertson, who starred in the series *Tales of Wells Fargo* in the 1950s. Dale liked a waitress who worked there, but he was a very bashful guy, so he sent me over to ask her if she could join us for dinner the next night. I gave her my phone number and the hotel room where I was staying.

Later that night, she was found dead in an alley with her throat slit. The only thing the police found on her was my phone number and hotel room. About four in the morning, the police kicked down my door and took me in for questioning. It took a while for them to find out what actually happened, and for the next couple of days I was very shaky. Dale Robertson and Dan Curtis started calling me "killer."

A week later the police arrested her ex-husband, a butcher, who confessed to the killing.

~~~

During the run of *Magnum, P.I.*, I had a few brushes with the law. One time, Peter Terranova, then vice president of Universal Studios, Tom Selleck, and I went to New York. I had heard all these stories about killings, muggings, and robberies in New York, so I brought a gun with me. It was a nine-millimeter Datodix, which had been a gift. I barely knew how to work it, but it had a clip in it, and I knew it was loaded. I kept it underneath my pillow in the suite.

I found out Robert Conrad was also in town. Conrad and I go back many years. He was the guy who started my career. Conrad has been very calm for several years now. But at that time, we were pretty rowdy. That night we made the rounds of several bars, until they all closed. When I dropped Conrad off at his hotel, it was daylight.

When I got back to my suite, I passed right out. Next thing I knew, the door burst open and there was a lot of commotion. It was Tom. He woke me up and pushed me into the shower. Then he took all of my clothes and threw them in my suitcases.

"We're gonna miss the damn plane!" he screamed.

A few minutes later, as I was running out of the suite, I remembered that the gun was under the bed pillow, so I grabbed it, opened a suitcase, and shoved it in. We took the limo, got stuck in traffic, and, sure enough, missed the private plane.

An American Airlines representative was sympathetic to our situation. She said, "There's a flight in seven minutes, and I've gotten all three of you on it. But you've gotta run your tails off. We'll take care of the luggage."

We ran through the metal detectors to the gate and boarded the plane. Selleck was in an aisle seat in first class and I was in the window seat next to him. I took Selleck's baseball hat off of his head and put it over my eyes.

"Aghhhhh," I groaned as I went right off to sleep, still drunk.

The next thing I knew, I heard someone saying, "Mr. Manetti?"

I looked up and said, "No autographs."

"Can we talk to you for a minute?" the guy insisted.

Standing up unsteadily, I said, "Sure." There were two very serious-looking men in suits and ties standing in the aisle. "I'll be right back," I said to Tom.

"Larry, I don't think so. Where's the gun?" Tom whispered.

"Don't worry about it," I said. "It's in my suitcase."

The minute I walked off the plane, they threw me on the ground, put my hands behind my back, handcuffed me, and read me my rights.

Airport personnel had found my loaded gun in the suitcase. The airport police arrested me. Someone had called the *National Enquirer*. Reporters were already storming through the airport, as the cops had me laying on the ground, facedown, unable to move.

149

"Please," I begged, "I can't be seen like this." Thankfully, the cop understood and called for a police cruiser.

In the meantime, Selleck and Terranova were still on the plane, and a woman had taken my empty first-class seat.

"Get out of that seat!" Terranova yelled. "That's my friend's!"

"But they told me to sit here," the woman said.

"They made a mistake," said Peter. "Get out of here."

The woman returned to her coach seat, but a few minutes later, Peter noticed that she was trying to sit in my seat again.

Peter motioned to a stewardess. "This is my friend's seat."

"Not anymore," said the stewardess. "He's staying in New York. He won't be coming with us."

While this was going on, I was walking to the police cruiser with my coat over my head. The cops were putting me in

Peter Terranova, former V.P. of Universal. He tried to hold my seat, but the cops had other plans for me.

the car and as I looked up, I saw Tom's face pressed against the window. He was waving bye-bye to me.

They took me to the police station, fingerprinted and booked me. I didn't know that they had a law called the Sullivan Act—if you get caught with a loaded gun, it's mandatory you're doing a year in jail. I went through the processing, and was told, "You're going to jail. No ifs, ands, or buts."

I was still drunk when I asked, "How long do I get?"

"You get a year," one of the cops responded.

"So what," I said in my wise-guy way, "I'll do a year on my head." Real dumb move.

I think the cop must've wanted to beat the daylights out of me. They took me to the holding area and handcuffed me to a metal bar. I was allowed one call. I called my wife, Nancy. She called Sonny Golden, my business manager, who was also Sinatra's business manager. She told Sonny to get in touch with

Sinatra and tell him to get me out of jail. Finally, they set me up with a lawyer.

The lawyer explained to me over the phone, "Here's the problem. They can't hold you where you are over the weekend, so they're going to move you to the 'tombs.'"

I found out "the tombs" is the oldest prison in the United States. There are literally tombs under the ground. I was terrified. The booze was starting to wear off. *Oh my God*, I was thinking, *how could this happen to me?*

A big, burly officer who seemed to be in charge came to talk to me. "I want to know why you did this," he said.

I told him the story about the gun and how I was frightened of New York. I told him the truth, too, that I was drunk.

"The last thing I need in my police station is an Italian movie star," the officer said. "We are going to give you a blood test. If you have any narcotics in your system, I can guarantee you, my friend, you're gonna go to jail for narcotics, on top of the Sullivan Act. But if you're clean, I'm releasing you, and I'll worry about the paperwork later. Maybe it was like this: You really tried to turn your gun in, but you got lost because you were inebriated, and you couldn't find the proper authority to turn weapons in to."

"Yes, sir," I said. "That's right."

I was given the blood test. I waited, and finally the officer came out and said, "You're clean. Congratulations. We're putting you on the next plane."

I got into a squad car, and was handed an airline ticket. I looked at the ticket and said, "Wait a minute. This is a coach ticket. I was flying first class."

The officer was incredulous. "Get the hell outta here, kid! I never want to see you again as long as I live!"

I was so ecstatic, I wanted to send him a new Corvette.

When I arrived at the L.A. airport, I called Nancy. She told me that Peter and Tom were on their way to Van Nuys Airport

151

to board a Lear jet to go back to New York for me. We reached them just in time as they were taxiing for take-off.

Meanwhile, I called a friend of mine at the *National Enquirer* and said, "Look, you can't print what happened. I've been good to you guys."

"Okay," the reporter said, "but we need a story."

I concocted a shark story that I said occurred while we were filming a *Magnum* segment. It went like this: I dove off a boat to save a tourist from drowning. As I was swimming, a twenty-two-foot tiger shark bumped me. I didn't know what it was. I saw this shadow, and it rolled over, and as it rolled over, I saw its teeth. Of course, I'd heard stories from the islanders in Hawaii that when a shark goes to strike someone, the shark's eyes close. So I kicked the shark in the face and swam my butt off. I saved the tourist and myself. The *National Enquirer* loved the story, and my friends had a ball with it since I can't swim and I'm afraid of goldfish.

I remember looking at my watch one time, yelling, "Oh God, I'm late!" I hopped into my newly purchased Porsche convertible and literally blew every red light, going around traffic, weaving in and out. Suddenly, in my rearview mirror, I saw a cop on one of those three-wheeled motor scooters. Well, there was no chance he was going to catch this car because it was a turbo, and I can drive. I figured I'd lose this cop real quick. I was on my way to Sergio's, the notorious watering hole and restaurant. The next thing I saw were four blue lights behind me, and then I saw even more of them. I started wheeling around corners until I came to the parking garage. I slid into it and drove all the way up to the third floor. I got out of the car and was running down the driveway when I saw all the cops positioned with their pistols out, screaming, "Freeze!" There must have been fifteen of them. They handcuffed me just as Tom was driving into the garage. He said, "Oh no,

Larry, what did you do now?" One of the policemen said, "He's going in. He sped away, tried to escape." But Tom talked to them and got me off, again. I was always in trouble and Tom was always getting me out of jackpots.

Another time, I was in the wrong place at the wrong time. I sat down at a dinner table with some guys who were of, let's say, nefarious character. The next day, the FBI came on the set and questioned me. The front pages of the local paper read something like, "*Magnum, P.I.* Star Brought in for Questioning for Racketeering." I thought that was goodbye for me. But the local government went to bat for me. They said, "Listen, you've got the wrong guy. This kid doesn't do that stuff." I was just sitting with some guys I'd known from Chicago who had unsavory reputations.

If Tom didn't have to be on the set early, he'd come along with me to Scruples Beach Club, which was owned by our dear friend, Fred Piluso. One night, while Tom was working, I stopped by and joined Freddie for a few cocktails. Afterwards, we jumped into his new Lamborghini and took off.

As we were driving through an intersection, a speeding car ran a red light and broadsided the Lamborghini on the passenger side. About four inches further in, and I would have been killed. The Lamborghini spun around and tipped over. We crawled out of the car quickly because we were afraid it would ignite and blow up.

Freddie ran over to the driver to see if he was all right. The guy was walking in the street, cursing at us, and we realized he was drunk. Freddie started pummeling the guy for wrecking his new Lamborghini. While they were fighting, the police arrived. They separated Freddie and the other driver and a heated confrontation ensued.

The drunk driver grew belligerent, but he wanted no more of Freddie, who was a six-foot-three, 220-pound ex-Army

Ranger. The guy figured he'd be safer taking a poke at me, so he took a swing and missed. I felt the wind go by my nose as I proceeded to throw a right-handed punch to his mouth. With that, the policeman, who had recognized me earlier, backhanded me and hit me in the chest. He was trying to break up the fight, but my instinct was to hit back, so I hit the cop square in his nose. I had gone too far. The cop grabbed me, saying to Fred, "I don't care who he is, he's going to jail."

We managed to straighten everything out at the police station later that night.

I was evicted numerous times during my eight years in Hawaii, and most of the time it was my fault. But at the very end, in 1988, I was totally innocent of a stunt which got me evicted. There was a knock at my door. When I answered, eight Honolulu policemen walked in, put me against the wall, and handcuffed me.

"You're under arrest," an officer informed me.

"For what?" I asked.

"You threatened the PBX telephone operator. You said that you were going to kill her."

"I never did that!" I cried. "They're stupid. They couldn't make the phone calls correctly. I'd call up and they'd get the wrong area codes. But I never threatened to kill anybody. You must be mistaken."

"So," the officer repeated, "you've never threatened to kill anybody?"

"No," I insisted.

"Well, we still have to take you in."

"All right," I said.

I yelled to Nancy in the kitchen to call my business manager, Sonny Golden, and tell him to get me an attorney. "Tell him if he screws up, I'll kill him!"

Chapter 10

Injuries, Charities, and Tragedies

he schedule took quite a toll on all of us, especially Tom, over the eight and a half years that we worked in Hawaii. It was brutal, fifteen hours a day in that heat. When the "candlelight" hit our eyes off the water, it was murder. The illumination of sunlight on the horizon is measured in "foot candles." We were so close to the equator that if we were in the sun and it was reflecting off the sand and water, it was hell. I can usually handle sun, but if I was outside in Hawaii for an hour lying by a pool, I'd get really burned. We had to wear a 25 SPF sunblock, or a total block. The sun was beating down on us every day. I still have little marks on my face where the sun discolored the pigmentation in my skin.

We had to worry about a lot of things, like what the sun was doing to our hair and to our eyes. Tom and I went to a doctor who prescribed special eye drops. Before we'd start shooting, I'd have to close my eyes or keep my eyes away from the sun so they wouldn't burn. For someone like me with light-colored eyes, it was rough. If you had a fair complexion, you had to worry about getting skin cancer. I had spots cut off my body, but luckily they weren't malignant.

We also had to be concerned about dehydrating because we were always sweating like crazy. For every shirt we wore in a scene, there were four duplicates. We'd be in the middle of a scene and have to change our shirts because they were drenched.

I can't complain too much, though, because Selleck really had it tougher. He made that show what it was—a big hit. Where other actors would whine and complain, and want this and that, he didn't. He took it all in stride. I give him a lot of respect for that.

I was injured a few times while I was filming *Magnum, P.I.* One time I fell and broke a rib on a sewer pipe, which I hadn't seen sticking up in the grass. Another time, one of the stunt men threw an actor on top of me during a fight scene, and I got my knee caught underneath a car. The knee went one way and I went the other. It wouldn't heal, so I finally had to have surgery on the torn cartilage. Fortunately, it improved enough that I was able to return to Hawaii to film a season-opening, two-hour *Magnum* set in Cambodia.

In another show, I was working with a little person. In one scene, the little person shimmied down a chimney to get into this house.

"You go through the window," the director told me.

"No," I insisted, "I'll go down the chimney, too. I'm thin enough."

Wrong. I got stuck in the chimney, and they had to break the bricks apart to get me out. I was all scraped up. After that, I went on a diet.

Selleck was hurt a lot, too, but you never heard about it. He never said a word.

One time, Tom was playing in a volleyball game at the Outrigger Canoe Club. He'd brought along his first wife Jackie's twelve-year-old son, Kevin, whom he had adopted.

After the game ended, they walked to the second level of the garage where Tom's Jeep was parked. Kevin loved cars, so Tom let him start it up. Trouble was, the Jeep was in gear as Kevin turned the ignition. Surprised when it jumped forward, he panicked and hit the gas. The Jeep crashed partway through the fence and dangled over the edge of the building, like a stunt scene from the show, before tumbling down two stories. Miraculously, neither Tom nor Kevin were seriously hurt.

A baseball broke Tom's finger during one episode, and he still has a little curve in that finger. He also had his nose broken and Achilles tendon ripped, and tore his hamstring in 1983 while rehearsing a softball sequence. Then he injured it even more while sprinting around the bases during the actual filming.

Tom was injured again while we were doing an episode with Lenny Montana, a very big guy who played Luca Brazzi in *The Godfather*. I played a waiter and had to learn Sicilian for this episode, which was about some Italian Mafia guys coming to Hawaii. In one scene, Tom came in to meet my character to get some information. Lenny Montana spotted Tom, and grabbed him around the neck from behind. I heard a cracking sound. Not realizing his own strength, Lenny had cracked something in Tom's neck, putting him out of commission for a few days.

John Hillerman never performed any stunts and was never injured. I don't remember Roger ever getting hurt during filming. However, he did get banged up participating in some sporting events a couple of times.

～～～

I'll never forget the call we received about a twelve-year-old boy named Mickey who was dying of brain cancer. He was a huge fan of the show, worshipped Tom Selleck, and wanted to meet the cast more than anything in the world. He lived in Honolulu. Mickey's parents, knowing he would die very soon, called Tom on the set one day. They told him the boy's doctors didn't expect him to make it through the afternoon.

Tom, Roger, and I were about to jump into a Jeep to go see the boy when one of the local policemen who provided security on the set offered to take us in his patrol car. He had us to the house in what seemed like seconds. As we walked in his room, Mickey looked up at us with the most excited smile I've ever seen. His whole face lit up. For a minute there, he didn't even look sick.

"Thank you!" was all he could manage.

Tom took hold of his hand. Mickey grabbed it hard and clutched it like he would never let go—all the while staring at Tom's ring, the kind we all wore on the show. The French cross on the ring was supposed to be the squadron symbol from our days together in Vietnam. The studio had spent a lot of money to have those rings custom made for us.

I took my ring off, placed it in Mickey's free hand, and tried not to cry as his life slipped away, his other hand still clutching Tom's. They buried little Mickey with my ring.

When we returned to the set, I had to leave. I kept thinking about Mickey, and about my own son, Lorenzo. We were all too choked up to get through our lines.

Years later, the studio had a replacement ring made for me.

~~~

We did numerous public appearances for charity. I was the spokesman at a charity event Tom couldn't attend because he was bogged down shooting a flashback episode about when he was in the Navy. For the episode, he wore a custom-made, Navy-white uniform—the dress whites. Tom felt guilty about not being at the event and called me. "You know," he said, "I can't, in good conscience, not do this. I'm going to shut down the production for a couple of hours. It's a good charity."

And it was for a good cause. It was for kids. We did everything for kids.

I was on the stage when Tom showed up. He had security and policemen around him. He walked over and hugged me. "What do you want me to do?" he asked.

"Auction something off," I said.

Some woman yelled out, "I want something from you, Tom."

"Okay, good," I said. "What do I hear for Tom's uniform?"

The audience went crazy. They shouted out bids. "Four thousand, five thousand, ten thousand."

I sold his uniform for $10,000 to a woman who seemed very pleased with her purchase.

Tom looked at me and said, "I'm not finished with it. We're still doing the show, Larry. Are you nuts?"

"We'll deliver it after the episode. Put your check up right now, lady."

When we finished shooting, Tom took the uniform off, and the lady picked it up.

During the winter of 1985, Selleck received the Variety Club of Hawaii's Heart of Show Business Award. The Variety Club is a nonprofit international organization that helps needy children. Tom always made himself available for public appearances like these.

Selleck felt people who are lucky enough to earn more than they need should share the wealth. He felt sharing was the essence of being human.

～～

Selleck, Freddie Piluso, and I were sitting in my condo one night in the early '80s when Freddie got a call from his dad, who had not phoned him in years. Freddie had been in Hawaii for twenty-seven years. His parents lived in Boca Raton, Florida.

His father told him that his mother had been diagnosed with a brain tumor and would need an operation as soon as possible. Freddie took the next flight to Florida. When he

Selleck and I with Robert Wagner, Freddie Piluso, and Mike Connors (Man-nix). Tom turned out to be a lifesaver when Freddie's mother was hospitalized.

arrived at the hospital, he was told that they couldn't operate on his mom because there was no place for her to recuperate after the operation. All of the beds in the intensive care units were filled. The hospital was packed. It was bizarre. She needed the operation or she would die, but they couldn't operate since they had no bed to put her in for her recovery and aftercare.

I felt terrible about it. I've known Freddie since we were kids in Chicago. When Freddie returned to the emergency room to see his mother, he found flowers that I had sent. She was always fond of me, and anything that I could do, I would do to keep her going.

The next day, there was still no bed. Freddie pleaded with the doctors and other hospital personnel, but was told that nothing could be done. There were other patients in the same bind, and until a bed opened up, there was no way they could operate. His mom was really looking bad, and Freddie kept begging the doctors, but to no avail.

In the meantime, I had sent a photo of Tom Selleck and me from the set of *Magnum* to Freddie's mom with an autographed note telling her to get well soon and that we loved her very much.

That night, as Freddie was pacing the floor at home, he received a call from the doctor, who told him to hurry to the hospital because they were going to operate on his mother. Freddie couldn't believe it

"But, Doc," he said, "I thought there were no beds. I thought nothing could be done."

"Well," said the doctor, "I went to see your mom, and I noticed the picture of Tom Selleck and Larry Manetti. My sister lives in Hawaii, and she dated Selleck. He was a real good guy, and he treated her right. So I'm going to find a way to take care of your mom even if we have to place a bed on the ceiling in the intensive care unit." Instead, they stuck an extra bed right by the nursing station.

The operation was successful and the aftercare was outstanding. Freddie's mother recovered. She's alive and well and very active to this day. Thank God for Tom Selleck.

Chapter 11

The Magnum Legacy

he premise of *Magnum, P.I.* was that Tom Magnum was a former Vietnam vet who became a private eye, and in return for room and board, he helped out with security at a grand estate in Hawaii belonging to novelist Robin Masters. The caretaker of the estate, Higgins, was an English gentleman who didn't always see eye-to-eye with Tom. Magnum's two buddies, who were with him in Vietnam, were my character, Rick, who ran the King Kamehameha Beach Club, and T. C., a helicopter pilot who gave tours around the Hawaiian islands. Rick and T. C. were always helping Magnum with his cases.

I always thought *Magnum, P.I.* was an excellent show, and apparently many other people agreed. We were nominated for three Emmys and other awards for best dramatic series. We received tremendous recognition when Tom was named Best Actor in a Dramatic Series at the Emmys in 1984. He was also nominated four other times.

Tom was also honored by the Vietnam Veteran Leadership Program because of his contributions and the contributions of the rest of the cast and crew of *Magnum, P.I.*, especially the writers and producers. The vets felt that the show gave viewers a greater understanding of Vietnam vets and also helped many veterans with delayed stress syndrome and other ailments they suffered due to the war. They were especially happy that the series involved Vietnam vets who dealt successfully with their memories of the war. Tom is an advocate of individual liberty, and he realizes the importance of our armed forces personnel.

After a few years, there were people who started talking about our show being among the best, or maybe *the* best, television series that was on at that time. I know there were people who said, "Oh no, it's not a *St. Elsewhere* or *Hill Street Blues*," but it was a lot more than just a "hunk" show. Sure, we had sex, violence, fast cars, guns, and beautiful tall men . . . and, of course, sexy, short men like me, but the show was much more than that.

Critics began taking us very seriously. We weren't just an everyday detective show. We dealt with character and values. It wasn't all just mystery and adventure. Our show was never predictable. One week could be a funny mystery, and the next week could be a serious two-parter set in Vietnam. I think what made *Magnum* so unique was the character development. Every now and then on the series, there'd be a story about how the characters ended up in Hawaii, and the past events that shaped their lives.

After a while, I stopped reading the reviews and critiques of *Magnum* because I never knew which way they were going. There were a number of critics who thought we were just showing off Thomas's good looks. Others felt we had a great ensemble cast, and enjoyed how the episodes went from comedy to thriller to drama to tears.

The shows that generated the most positive reaction were the ones dealing in some way with Vietnam. Many critics felt that the entire series dealt with Vietnam by showing what happened to these guys after they came back from the war, how they adjusted to life; albeit in Hawaii, which wasn't exactly as difficult as coming home to the urban mainland of the United States. Here was Magnum, an officer who woke up one day in his early thirties and realized that he had missed a lot of his life, especially his twenties. Once a serious career Naval officer, he became a carefree private detective in Hawaii. Viewers enjoyed the show's flashbacks to Southeast Asia because it showed Magnum in a more serious and heroic mode, as opposed to the laid-back islander in his baseball cap and shorts.

On the other hand, there were some critics who did not like the way we portrayed the Vietnam situation. Our characters did not return from Vietnam with delayed stress syndrome, Agent Orange, or other problems, like many GIs. They served their country, came home, and were proud of it. Whereas many earlier television programs and films had depicted only the bitterness and emotional hassles of Vietnam vets, *Magnum, P.I.* showed that things could be different. It was a much more positive portrayal of the Vietnam War and Vietnam vets.

Actually, Don Bellisario said that he treated the *Magnum* characters not as Vietnam vets, but more like returning World War II vets. Our characters did harbor some anger and disillusionment as a result of the war, but they didn't really suffer from post-traumatic stress syndrome or anything like that. They had memories, bad and good, so they were more like World War II veterans.

I don't think that Magnum would have been a private detective if he hadn't been in Vietnam. I don't think my character would have been someone who skated on the edge of illicit activities, the rackets, or the Hawaiian underworld if it wasn't for Vietnam. And, of course, T. C., who flew the tourist helicopter, picked up his skills in Vietnam. Even Higgins, who ran the estate, was a retired British Army officer, and had been involved in a number of wars.

We were all in a semi-panic when *The Cosby Show* came on opposite us on Thursday nights and started beating us in the ratings. We were entering our sixth season, and some people thought we were declining. We figured we might have to do some creative casting to improve the ratings. There was talk that Jack Lord, who played McGarrett on *Hawaii Five-O*, would come in and guest star every now and then. But it never happened. There was also talk of putting more scantily clad women on the show, but that wasn't what *Magnum* was about, and we weren't going to change our image like that.

At about the same time, we decided to downplay some of the Vietnam stuff, even though it was a favorite of many fans of the show. We figured it was best not to overdo it. Having established ourselves as proud to be Americans, there was no reason to run with it unless we had a really good script.

Once, in *TV Guide*, Selleck talked about how many people perceived Magnum as a silly, laid-back guy, when he truly had a darker, more serious side. If you harmed his friends, he'd kill you, literally. Selleck referred to the two-parter, "Did You See the Sun Rise?" which received the most critical acclaim of any *Magnum, P.I.* episode. It was one of Don Bellisario's best scripts. At the very end, Tom killed a Russian diplomat in cold blood. The diplomat had killed Magnum's friend. Magnum just said, "Ivan, you'll never see the sunrise." Then he blew him away. Thousands of letters poured in to the network praising that show.

However, not everybody loved *Magnum, P.I.* Former world heavyweight boxing champion Ingamar Johanson called our show a joke in an *Esquire* magazine article.

"Either you are a tough show or a funny show. You shouldn't be both," he said.

Maybe Floyd Patterson hit him harder than I thought.

Our show was a great draw for tourists. I believe that tourism jumped dramatically because of the show. People visited

It felt great to be on a hit show, and we all appreciated the fans.

Hawaii just to get a peek at us or to watch us filming. We made special arrangements for the tourists so that nobody would go home disappointed. There was only one tour company which had approval from our studio to bus tourists to the set of *Magnum, P.I.* They would bring hundreds and hundreds of *Magnum* fans to the set. We'd pose for pictures, say hello, and sign autographs. Tom was especially cooperative. He would accommodate the fans even if there were five sessions a day because he never wanted to disappoint anyone; and it was always on his own time when he could have been resting. He was great.

During our years in Honolulu, especially when *Magnum* was at the top of the ratings, many people equated Hawaii with the series. Everywhere you looked in Hawaii, you'd see a smiling Selleck on posters and on T-shirts. Tourists would point up at T. C.'s chopper whirling around over Honolulu. And when they came out to the set, their eyes would bulge staring at the red Ferrari parked at the Robin's Nest Estate.

Unfortunately some tourists could go a little bananas, trying to scale the walls of the estate to get into the house, and even stealing tree branches as souvenirs.

Tom had bodyguards around to control the female fans since they all wanted to be photographed with him, and there were almost stampedes at times.

Tourists from all over the U.S. were flocking to Hawaii because of *Magnum* and the way the show portrayed the beautiful blue skies, clear water, and laid-back atmosphere. In its time, *Hawaii Five-O* drew a lot of tourists to Hawaii, too. I will admit that *Hawaii Five-O* probably showed more of the geography, but I think *Magnum* increased tourism much more. Of course, the economy was different in the '80s, and people were spending more money.

During the years after *Magnum* ended, tourism in Hawaii declined dramatically. Many locals will admit that it was because of the loss of *Magnum*.

There are always tourists who decide to visit Hawaii six months or a year in advance, but the key to tourism is the Frequent Independent Travelers (FITs), who, on a whim, will decide impulsively to take off for some exciting or exotic locale. In the '80s, there were thousands and thousands of people every month who watched *Magnum, P. I.* and said, "Hey, let's go there! Let's go to Hawaii!" When they arrived, they immediately wanted to see where *Magnum* was filmed.

Magnum, P. I. also made people more aware of Ferraris. Word was that sales tripled. I was told that 80 percent of the people who bought red Ferraris at Shelton Motors in Honolulu were inspired to buy them because of the show. The real Ferrari, a 1982 308-GTSi which cost $63,000 at the time, was a two-seater, V-8 fuel-injection rear engine. It got ten miles to a gallon, and topped out at about 120 miles per hour.

Magnum, P.I. is now shown in over 140 countries. We're in syndication paradise. From what I understand, we're on at least once or twice a day in every major city in the United States.

Chapter 12

Life after Magnum

I really love speed, and I think that's what got me involved with car racing. It probably goes back to when I was very young and used to exercise thoroughbred racehorses for a buddy of my father's. I became pretty good, and I really enjoyed riding fast. I probably could have been a jockey except I was too big and heavy, so I switched my speed lust to cars. About three or four years into *Magnum*, I decided to take some lessons in car racing because I fantasized about entering the Grand Prix. I decided I didn't want to be a professional, but I wanted to race from time to time; like Paul Newman was doing, becoming a pretty accomplished racecar driver.

I took my Ferrari to Bob Bondurant's School of High Performance Driving in Sonoma, California. This was during the third year of the series. I received the classroom instruction, then got onto the track. I drove about 120 or 130 miles per hour, and was put through all the paces. It was fun. I think Bondurant gave me a C+ overall, but he told me that he graded pretty tough and not to think that was a poor grade. I did get an "A" in guts from Bondurant, though. Unfortunately, because we filmed *Magnum* nine months out of the year, I was unable to return to car racing.

It used to be that I would eat just about anything. I loved meat, potatoes, and candy. I would buy ten Snickers bars at a time. I also consumed alcohol before, during, and after dinner sometimes. Once I settled in Hawaii and finally got into the swing of things there with the healthy lifestyle, culture, and climate, I made the big switch. I stayed away from red meat, chocolate, and wine, and started to eat fish, pasta, and fruit.

I had never been a fish eater before. It smelled too fishy, and I didn't see the point in eating it. But the fish in Hawaii was always fresh and tasted mild and somewhat meaty. I guess it was the way it was prepared more than anything.

Instead of going for candy in the afternoon like I used to, I would freeze packages of pasta in microwaveable bags. When there was a break on the set I would go to the trailer and microwave the pasta. It gave me the energy I never had up until then. For dinner, I was eating sushi, broiled fish, and vegetables. I found that changing my diet allowed me to sleep much better, too.

I came from a family that enjoyed food and cooking and, as a result, I learned a lot about recipes and ingredients. During *Magnum*, magazines like *Us, Your Health*, and the *National Star* wrote some articles about me involving food and cooking. Following that, I got to do a spot on a live TV show with Robert Morley called *Celebrity Chefs*.

I had to be up at six to be on the set. But I had been out the night before with Anthony Quinn until two o'clock in the morning, and when I returned to my hotel, I bumped into some people I knew, and wound up in one of their suites until four. So I arrived on the set tired and hungover, with no idea what I was in for. The producer dressed me in a white apron with sleeves and this goofy white hat. I was supposed to prepare

Hawaiian food using exotic ingredients with Hawaiian names that were difficult to pronounce, especially with a hangover.

I kept asking where Robert Morley was, but no one seemed to know. He finally arrived three seconds before air time. I was standing there cooking over a blazing fire when he came flying in. "*Celebrity Chefs*, ladies and gentlemen," he announced. "Today's guest is Larry Manetti!"

"Good morning," I said. "How are you, Robert?"

The director was motioning for Morley to move further to the right so he'd be on camera, and I was standing right next to him. The man weighed over 280 pounds, and as he moved, I realized that he was unstable. He lost his balance and toppled over me, and I fell onto the stovetop.

As I got up from the stove, I realized that I was on fire. In a frenzy, I tried to put it out by fanning myself with the tall white hat. Robert Morley was standing there watching me burn, laughing uncontrollably. Then he sprayed me with a fire extinguisher on live TV.

173

"Ladies and gentlemen," Morley said calmly, as he stared directly into the camera, "this young man has a tendency to panic while cooking Hawaiian food."

A few months later, I was asked to appear on *Live with Regis and Kathie Lee* to cook my specialty, Steak Lorenzo. First, I heated the oil in a large black iron pan. While I started preparing the ingredients, Regis decided that he wanted to cook with me. We started fooling around, doing one-on-one jokes. I turned around, thinking I was reaching for the onions, and instead, stuck my hand right into the hot pan. The pain was excruciating, but I didn't dare scream.

"Your hand is in the frying pan!" yelled Regis.

"I know," I replied, matter-of-factly.

Then I proceeded to put butter on my hand, which, I discovered later, is the last thing you should do when you have a bad burn.

"Well," I continued, "I guess the only thing to do now that I've cooked my hand is to eat it."

I stacked all of the ingredients on my right hand and pretended I was eating it. The audience was in hysterics. When I got off stage, I fainted, and was taken directly to the hospital. Interestingly, Steak Lorenzo is included in Regis and Kathie Lee's cookbook, *Cooking with Regis and Kathie Lee*, and it includes the step where I stuck my hand in the hot frying pan.

∼∼∼

I spent some time at Willie Nelson's ranch in Texas several years ago because we were going to do a film together. He wanted to meet me and make sure that we got along. I stayed in one of the condominiums on his land for three or four days, and I had a wonderful time. He was a sweetheart of a guy.

A couple of weeks later Willie was in Los Angeles rehearsing for a concert at the Universal Amphitheater. I visited him in his motor home for about an hour.

Willie Nelson is a great guy, but he learned the hard way that I'm just not a fan of country western music!

"Be my guest tonight," he insisted, handing me a ticket to the concert. "Later," he added, "we'll meet for a late snack."

I told him that after the concert I had plans and there was no way that I could have dinner. What Willie didn't know was that I am just not a country western fan, and I didn't want to sit through a long show. So I pretended that I would go to the show, figuring he'd never know the difference. I threw the ticket out of the car window on my way home.

Was he in for a shock! That evening, in the middle of the concert, Willie Nelson introduced me to the crowd.

"Ladies and gentlemen, the costar of *Magnum, P.I.*, Larry Manetti!"

The spotlight flashed on my seat because Willie had given the lighting director the seat number. A black man who had found the ticket was sitting there, blinded by the light, as Willie told him to stand up and say hello to the audience. The poor guy slowly rose, and everybody started laughing.

In the mid-1980s, I formed a company called Lorenzo Productions for the purpose of producing feature films, television movies, TV series, and other projects. The first film I wanted to make, *Kids in Charge*, was about child abuse. I was going to have Barbara Sinatra star in it with me, and the proceeds would go to the Barbara Sinatra Children's Center. We never got it made. The rejection of the project was no different than being rejected from an acting job. So, undaunted, I persevered.

Next, I bought the rights to two books, *Bad Guys* and *The Booster*, written by Eugene Izzi. Both were on the bestseller's list. These projects also failed. So I bought another book from Eugene Izzi called *The Take*, which was number four on the bestseller's list. Surprise! This effort did manage to result in a made-for-TV movie. It aired on the USA cable network and starred me, Lisa Hartman, and Ray Sharkey, who passed away recently from AIDS.

Later, I co-produced a television series based on the Robert DeNiro movie *Midnight Run*, with George Gallo, the original writer and producer. We did thirteen episodes. Currently, I'm having a script written for a project called *Sunset Strip Wars* about the battle for L.A. by gangsters after Bugsy Siegel died.

In 1995, I was asked to join the cast of the series *Marker*, starring Richard Grieco. Grieco is a good friend, a wonderful guy, and a great actor (*If Looks Could Kill, Mobsters*). Another friend, John Ashley, was the producer. At one time he was a very successful actor. He did all of the beach party movies with Frankie Avalon, went on to own a chain of theaters, and then became the producer of *The A-Team*. Andrew Stevens, also a friend of mine and an actor, who was at one time married to Kate Jackson, was directing an episode of *Marker* that I was in. All of the guys decided: Let's get Manetti again.

My character was a real tough homicide cop by the name of Lieutenant Oserman, a cross between James Cagney and Columbo. While I was reading the script, they were all secretly watching me as I sat on a chaise longue by the swimming pool.

I came to a part in the script where another cop said to Marker, "You'll never believe this, but somebody saw Lieutenant Oserman coming out of one of those S & M bars, you know what I mean, man? He came out in drag with full makeup, a wig, high heels, and a dress."

"No, it can't be," said Marker.

And the cop replied, "I'm telling you, it's true."

I thought they must have messed up. It had to be somebody else. The writers must have put my character's name in by mistake. No big deal. I continued reading.

The script was about a rock star, heavily into drugs, who had flipped out and wanted to commit suicide by hiring a hit man to kill him. My character's job was to find this hit man and capture him.

At the end of the script, the hit man shot the rock star. My character ran over and grabbed the rock star as he lay dying, caressing his hair and holding his face. Then my character said, "Don't worry, sweetheart, everything will be all right. I'm here to hold your hand."

I thought, *What the hell kind of dialogue is this? My character doesn't talk like this. I'd be yelling, "Call 911! Move your ass!"*

Then Marker came over and said, "Jesus! What's going on? What are you doing, Lieutenant Oserman? This is unbelievable!"

"Can't two guys show their true affection?" my character responded, weeping. "This is 1995. The world is a new place to live. We love each other."

I freaked out.

"That's it!" I screamed. "I'm out of here. I ain't playing this guy. They can go screw themselves!"

I took the script and threw it across the pool. Then I ran over to the house phone, called United Airlines, and booked myself a flight back to L.A. Still fuming, I called John Ashley in his office. He, of course, was running back to get the call after watching me go bananas by the pool. He answered the phone on the tenth ring.

"Did you read this script?" I bellowed.

"Of course I did," he answered, calmly, but out of breath.

"Are you nuts?" I asked. "I couldn't play this kind of guy! Whoever wrote this is an imbecile!"

"But Larry," he said, "an actor should be able to act. You should be able to modify your role."

"Well, I'm not doing it!" I steamed. "I'm on a plane."

I hung up. When I lose my temper I really go crazy. I ran into my room, grabbed a chair, and smashed it against the wall.

Just then, Grieco, Ashley, and Stevens came rushing into the room. They were all laughing.

"What's so funny?" I asked.

They told me that they had set me up and rewritten the script. I smiled, realizing that they had gotten me.

A month later, I received a bill from the studio for $200 for the broken chair.

≈≈≈

An actor's life isn't always all that it's made out to be, even after you've done a successful series. When you're working, it's wine and roses. When you're not, it's depressing. You call your agent every day to see if someone has a project for you. There's a lot of rejection. Instead of feeling despondent or spending my days playing golf, I decided to find something else to occupy my time and utilize my skills.

At first, I tried to become a spokesman or marketeer for a big corporation, but nothing significant panned out. Then, lo and behold, the Desert Inn Hotel in Las Vegas contacted me and asked if I was interested in being one of their representatives. Because of my recognizability as an actor, they thought

I guest starred on several series after Magnum, *including* Quantum Leap, *with Scott Bakula.*

I'd be good at increasing business for their casino. They said they'd get me a gambling license so that I could send "players" on a complimentary basis to the Desert Inn. As a reward or commission, I would receive three percent of their wins or losses. It sounded great, so I took the job.

A few months later, I received a telephone call from one of the executives at the new MGM Grand Hotel asking me to leave the Desert Inn and work for them. I told them I wasn't interested, but they continued to call. About a month and a half later, a couple of MGM executives flew in and took my wife and me to dinner.

"Look," they said, "we're really interested in you, and we'd like for you to run our Los Angeles marketing office. You'll have five people working under you and there'll be a six-figure salary with perks. You know, all expenses paid..."

I thought about it, and the next week I flew into Las Vegas to meet their key people and check out the hotel. I was very impressed.

"But," I cautioned them, "the problem is I'm an actor and my acting career comes first. I can't take this job if it will consume all of my time. I need flexibility."

"No, no," they assured me, "we're hiring you because of your face, your recognizability, your charm... You know a lot of high rollers, people who make a good living, and you could also sway gamblers from other hotels."

They assured me that I would not have to be in the office or be a hands-on guy. My main function would be to simply go out to bars and restaurants and charm the elite into gambling at the MGM Grand. To sweeten the deal even more, they promised me a bonus of 40 percent of anything over 1.5 million dollars a year that was referred from the L.A. office.

I took the job, opened the office, and spent a lot of time there—more than I should have—and I did much better than they expected. Every month the profits escalated.

After some time, I went to Hawaii to film *Marker*. While I was there, I sent the MGM Grand a lot of business from Hawaii. I wined and dined people there and even interviewed staff for an MGM Grand office opening in Hawaii. When *Marker* ended, I returned to L.A. and concentrated on their office again.

Then I had a movie offer. When I informed my MGM bosses, they frowned on it and told me not to take it.

"Right now is a bad time," they said. "The office is really starting to take off. We don't want you to go."

I agreed not to do the film. But when I tried to get out of my verbal commitment with the production company, they threatened to sue me for $100,000. I relayed this to the executives at MGM, but they were persistent, "We don't want you to go."

So I made a deal with the production company. They were nice enough to let me off the hook as long as I understood that they expected me to come through without any hesitation the next time they needed me. That was "strike one."

"Strike two" came when I was offered a move called *Exit* in Florida for Republic Studio. I informed MGM that I wanted to do this one for sure. They agreed, but wanted a written memo explaining my decision. I wrote the memo, but before they signed off on it, they stipulated that I could only go for two weeks, and my salary would be docked during that time. I didn't think that was right, but I let it slide.

On the fourth day of shooting in Florida, I received a "strike three" call saying that the MGM president was very upset and felt that I had not acted wisely in taking the movie offer instead of staying at the L.A. office. He wanted to offer me a new deal, cutting my salary drastically and putting me on straight commission. This meant that I'd lose my executive position.

The paradox is that MGM hired me because I was a recognizable actor, and to continue that recognition I needed to

Tom and I still like to get together with friends for poker—here we are with Dennis Farina, Freddie Piluso (owner of Scruples), and our makeup man Lon Bently.

be seen on TV and/or in the movies. But MGM wanted me in the office and frowned on my taking time off to film a TV series or movie. This meant that people would start to forget me, which made no sense. But the good news was that the Desert Inn found out and asked me to come back.

As I mentioned earlier, Tom and I both feel that there would be tremendous interest in a *Magnum, P.I.* feature-length movie. Tom has stated publicly over the years that he was really peeved with Universal Studios because he felt they didn't support the idea. After successful feature films were made based on older TV series like *The Fugitive* and *Maverick*, it seemed like a no-brainer to do *Magnum.* Tom Clancy, who is a good friend of Tom's, thinks it is such a great idea that he offered to write the screenplay. The story line has already been developed. It's about Magnum going back to the Navy amid a nuclear threat in North Korea. Clancy is very gung-ho about it.

Recently, ownership of Universal changed hands, and it appeared that *Magnum, P.I.—The Movie* was a go. But for some reason, the powers-that-be think that it's better to do four two-hour TV *Magnum* movies first. Tom is adamantly opposed to that idea.

James Garner has asked Tom numerous times to recreate the role of Lance White, which he was playing when I first met him years ago. If Tom agreed, it would be a two-hour *Rockford Files* TV movie. Tom has the utmost respect for Garner and feels that the Magnum character and Rockford were similar in a number of ways.

Tom did a number of episodes on the highly rated series *Friends* as Monica's lover. In 1998, he starred in a new sitcom, *The Closer*. I thought Tom was great in the movie *In and Out* with Kevin Kline, for which he received rave reviews.

The past few years have been great for me. Besides guest appearances in the TV series *JAG* and *NYPD Blue*, I also did feature films. I was in the following four movies: *Top of the World* with Dennis Hopper and Peter Weller; *Scarred City* with Chazz Palminteri, Stephen Baldwin, and Tia Carrere; *Hijack* with Jeff Fahey and Ernie Hudson; and *The Accountant* with Michael Madsen and Rob Lowe. I credit my agent, Jack Gilardi of the ICM Agency, for helping me to land these recent roles.

I also own Duet, a very hip club in Westwood with Chris Mallick. Naturally, I've been doing a lot of the cooking, and when I'm not in the kitchen, I'm out front greeting customers. The crowd is usually younger, but they must still watch *Magnum, P.I.* reruns because they often call me Rick.

Appendix

Larry's Favorite Recipes for the Stars

I first became interested in cooking while watching my dad work in the kitchen of a couple of taverns he owned when I was young.

However, it wasn't until my late teens when I was working at Sportsmen Park Race Track that I really learned the craft of cooking. Every time I got into trouble in my job working the betting window, I'd be sent (actually suspended) to clean up the private dining room kitchen.

I'd watch these great Italian and Greek cooks who prepared food for the jockeys, trainers, owners, and visiting dignitaries. They eventually let me experiment with simple dishes and gradually introduced me to intricate recipes. I got hooked, and have been for over thirty-five years.

STEAK LORENZO

Steak Lorenzo is included in Regis and Kathie Lee's cookbook, Cooking with Regis and Kathie Lee. Nancy and I prepared it and took it to Robert Wagner and Jill St. John's home one night when they were both sick, and it became one of their favorite meals.

> 2 to 4 tablespoons olive oil
> 2 tablespoons butter
> 2 cloves garlic, finely chopped
>   Fresh or dried rosemary leaves to taste
>   Dried sage leaves to taste
> 2 New York or club steaks (about 1 pound
>   total) cut into bite-size pieces
> 3 tablespoons red wine

185

In a skillet, heat the butter and two tablespoons of the oil over medium/high heat. Add the garlic and cook for two to three minutes, or until the garlic is lightly browned, stirring constantly. Remove the garlic.

Crush the rosemary and sage between your fingertips to release oils and add to the skillet. Cook for one to two minutes, stirring constantly.

Season the steak with salt and pepper. Increase the heat to high, add the steak, cook for two to four minutes, or until steak is cooked to the desired degree of doneness, stirring constantly.

Add the wine, cover, cook for one minute, and serve.

TURKEY CUTLETS

This is a favorite dish of Don Bellisario and Frankie Avalon. Don likes to eat at my house. We spend the evening reminiscing about all the old series we worked on together. Don is also an excellent chef.

Frankie Avalon and I go way back, and we share the same agent, Jack Gilardi. Frankie likes his food spicy, and I always add Giardincera (a hot vegetable mix) or crushed red peppers.

2 pounds turkey cutlets
2 cups Romano cheese
6 cups bread crumbs
4 eggs, beaten
4 cloves garlic, chopped
Salt to taste
Pepper to taste
4 tablespoons olive oil

Place one turkey cutlet between two pieces of waxed paper and lightly pound. Repeat with each cutlet.

In a shallow bowl, beat the eggs.

On a separate platter, combine the bread crumbs and cheese.

Dredge the turkey in the eggs and then into the bread crumb mixture.

Heat a skillet with two tablespoons of olive oil and half the chopped garlic. Brown the garlic until golden and remove from the skillet.

Place the breaded turkey in the skillet and add salt and pepper. Cook on each side for three minutes or until golden.

Repeat the browning of the garlic in the oil when you are halfway through the cutlets, as this will freshen the taste of the garlic.

CHICKEN CACCIATORE

Tom Selleck is a chicken lover, so any entree I cook with chicken, he loves. I'll usually even deliver it to his home. Every holiday season, during my annual Christmas party, Tom will stop by, always counting on dining on a huge platter of Chicken Cacciatore.

4 pounds chicken, cut into pieces
4 tablespoons olive oil
1 medium onion, chopped
3 cloves garlic, minced
1½ cups fresh tomatoes, peeled and chopped
1 tablespoon tomato paste
½ teaspoon oregano
Salt to taste
½ cup dry red wine
1 cup sliced mushrooms
1 cup black pitted olives
1 cup butter beans, drained
2 tablespoons parsley, minced

Saute onions and garlic in olive oil until just golden. Do not burn.

In the same pan, brown chicken pieces. Add salt, pepper, and oregano.

Keep turning until evenly browned. This will take about fifteen minutes.

Add tomatoes, tomato paste, and wine.

Cook covered for thirty minutes, then add mushrooms, beans, olives, and parsley.

Continue cooking another twenty minutes or until chicken is tender.

PASTA FAGIOLI

*I took this dish over to Frank Sinatra's house quite often. He liked
lots of salt in the pasta water and he didn't like garlic.*

> 2 handfuls of Romano or Parmesan cheese
>   (optional)
> ¼ cup olive oil
> ¼ stick butter
> 2 bulbs of garlic, peeled and chopped
> 1 onion, chopped
> 3 stalks of celery, chopped
> 3 15-ounce cans white northern beans
>   retaining juice
> 2 15-ounce cans red kidney beans retaining
>   juice
> 5 15-ounce cans chicken broth or stock
> 1 ham hock
> ¼ pound prosciutto (Italian ham)
> ¼ pound pancetta (Italian bacon)
> 1 handful chopped parsley
> ¼ cup red wine
> 1 pound pasta (small shells)
>   Salt and pepper to taste

Saute garlic in olive oil until golden, then remove and discard
the garlic.

Brown the pancetta, then add the onions, celery, and butter. Allow onions to caramelize.

Add the kidney beans and white northern beans with juice
from cans. Simmer for twenty minutes.

Add ham hock, salt, pepper, and wine.

After three minutes, add prosciutto, parsley, and chicken broth.

Simmer for one hour uncovered.

Boil water in a separate pot, and cook the pasta al dente.

Add pasta to soup when cooked.

If desired, add two handfuls of Romano or Parmesan cheese.

ESCAROLE AND BEAN SOUP

My "home boy" from Chicago, Dennis Farina, usually spends his free time at my home when he's in Los Angeles filming. His last couple of movies, Get Shorty *and* That Old Feeling, *have done very well. He has a new TV series,* Buddy Faro. *Dennis refers to my house as "the best Italian restaurant in L.A.!"*

⅛ cup olive oil
1 bulb garlic, chopped
2 bunches escarole (Italian lettuce), chopped
3 cans white northern beans retaining juice
⅛ stick butter (optional)
Crushed red pepper to taste
Salt to taste
Black pepper to taste
2 handfuls Parmesan cheese
6 cans chicken broth or stock

Saute garlic until golden, then discard. Add oil, red pepper, salt, black pepper, and beans with juice.

Simmer twenty minutes.

Add escarole and cook until it is wilted, then add chicken broth.

Simmer another twenty minutes. Turn off heat and add the cheese, stirring well.

LINGUINE AND CLAM SAUCE

Ernest Borgnine has a hearty appetite. When we are watching a director's cut of The Wild Bunch, *and he's explaining the film scene by scene, I cook enough linguine and clam sauce for four!*

    1 pound linguine
    ⅓ cup olive oil
    ½ stick butter (optional)
    3 cloves garlic, pressed or minced
    4 6.5-ounce cans minced clams,
        retaining liquid
    1 teaspoon dried oregano
    ¼ teaspoon pepper or to taste
    2 tablespoons chopped fresh parsley

191

In a large pot of boiling water, cook linguine until just tender. In a small saucepan, heat oil and butter until the butter melts. Add garlic, cook until golden. Stir in clams with liquid, oregano, pepper, and parsley. Cook until heated, about five minutes.

Drain linguine, return to pot. Add clam sauce. Toss and serve with grated Romano cheese.

ITALIAN BEEF STEW

My good buddy and costar, Roger Mosley, actually got me think-ing about eating fish when we were in Hawaii. During the meal breaks when we were shooting Magnum, *he'd always reach for the seafood while I went for the meat.*

But now that we're back in the states, when Roger and his wife come over, I make them Italian Beef Stew. They like it so much they always ask for a doggie bag to go.

However, I must confess that this recipe is really my mother's!

½ cup olive oil
3 pounds chuck, cut in medium-size cubes
½ onion, chopped
½ glass of red wine
1 large celery stalk, chopped
6 carrots, peeled and chopped
1 6-ounce can tomato paste
4 potatoes, precooked and cut into pieces
1 6-ounce can mushrooms
Salt and pepper to taste

Brown meat in olive oil.

Add salt and pepper to taste.

Add onions until the meat and onions are brown, about fifteen minutes.

Add red wine and simmer for five minutes.

Add celery and carrots. Simmer for fifteen minutes.

Dissolve tomato paste in three cups of water. Add to stew.

Simmer until meat is fully cooked, twenty to twenty-five minutes.

In the last five minutes of cooking, add the mushrooms and precooked potatoes.

BRUSCHETTA WITH TOMATOES, BEANS, AND FRESH HERBS

Milton Berle and his wife Lorna fell in love with this special appetizer I prepared for Nancy's birthday party at our home. The Bruschetta was arranged by the bar, and between card tricks, jokes, and a pre-Castro cigar, Milton ate to his heart's delight.

TOPPING INGREDIENTS

 1 cup ripe beefsteak tomatoes,
  seeded and diced
 ¾ cup canned white northern beans,
  drained
 ¼ cup cucumbers, seeded and diced
 2 tablespoons green onion, thinly sliced
 1 tablespoon chopped fresh basil *or*
  1½ teaspoons dried basil
  Freshly ground pepper to taste

193

BRUSCHETTA INGREDIENTS

 8 slices country-style white bread,
  each 2½ inches wide and ½ inch thick
 1 large clove garlic, cut in half
 4 teaspoons extra virgin olive oil

TOPPING PREPARATION

In a bowl, combine all the topping ingredients.

Toss well, cover, and refrigerate for at least one to two hours or for up to two days to allow the flavors to blend.

BRUSCHETTA PREPARATION

Preheat broiler.

Arrange the bread slices on a rack on a broiler pan and broil for two minutes.

Turn the bread slices over and continue to cook until golden, one to two minutes longer.

Remove from heat and rub a cut side of the garlic clove over one side of each warm slice of bread.

Brush each bread slice with ½ teaspoon of olive oil.

Mound an equal amount of the topping on the garlic-brushed side of each bread slice.

Serve immediately.

ZABAIONE

I've made Zabaione for Robert Conrad at my home and at his home in Bear Valley. It's the only dessert Bob will eat because he is such a fitness addict, and I prepare it with mostly egg whites.

 5 egg whites
 1 whole egg
 2 tablespoons sugar
 ½ cup Marsala

Combine the egg whites, whole egg, and sugar in the top of a double boiler above simmering water.

Beat the mixture with a wire whisk or a rotary beater until it is pale yellow and fluffy.

Gradually add the Marsala, stirring continually until the Zabaione is thick enough to hold its shape in a spoon. This may take about ten minutes.

Spoon the Zabaione into individual dessert bowls or large-stemmed glasses.

Serve while still hot.

MINESTRONE

This has long been a favorite of Mike Connors' (who starred in Mannix *for eight years). The first time I ever saw Mike on TV was in the early sixties. He was a guest attorney on* Perry Mason *when Raymond Burr was out due to minor surgery.*

When Mike was down with the flu, I brought over my Minestrone. After he recovered, he referred to it as "Italian Chicken Soup."

½ cup dry white beans
4 tablespoons butter
1 cup green peas
1 cup zucchini, diced
1 cup carrots, diced
1 cup potatoes, diced
⅓ cup celery, thinly sliced
2 ounces salt pork, diced
2 tablespoons chopped onions
½ cup chopped leeks
2 cups canned whole-pack tomatoes
   coarsely chopped, drained
2 quarts chicken stock (fresh or canned)
1 bay leaf and 2 parsley sprigs tied together
1 teaspoon salt
   Fresh ground pepper to taste
½ cup white raw rice

Bring one quart of water to a bubbling boil in a heavy 3- to 4-quart saucepan.

Add the beans and boil briskly for two minutes.

Remove pan from heat and let beans soak undisturbed in the water for one hour.

Return the pan to the stove and simmer uncovered over low heat for one to one and one-half hours, until beans are tender.

Drain beans thoroughly and set them aside in a bowl.

Melt the butter over moderate heat in a heavy 10- to 12-inch skillet.

When the foam subsides, add the peas, zucchini, carrots, potatoes, and celery, tossing the vegetables constantly with a wooden spoon for two to three minutes. Set aside.

Render the salt pork by frying in a 6- to 8-quart soup pot, stirring frequently.

When the pork is crisp, lift out, reserving fat, and set aside to drain on paper towels.

Stir the onions and leeks into the remaining fat from the pork, and cook, stirring constantly for seven or eight minutes.

Stir in the tomatoes, the vegetables from the skillet, the chicken stock, the bay leaf and parsley sprigs, salt, and pepper.

197

Bring the soup to a boil over high heat.

Reduce heat and simmer partially covered for twenty-five to thirty minutes.

Remove and discard bay leaf and parsley sprigs.

Add the rice, white beans, and salt pork.

Cook fifteen to twenty minutes longer or until rice is cooked.

Sample the soup and adjust the salt and pepper to taste.

Serve, passing a bowl of grated Parmesan cheese to sprinkle on top of the soup.

Episode Guide

agnum, P.I. aired on CBS from December 1980 to May 1988 for 162 episodes (including the pilot and two-parters). It starred Tom Selleck as Thomas Sullivan Magnum, John Hillerman as Jonathan Higgins, Roger E. Mosley as T. C., and me, Larry Manetti, as Rick.

The series was created by Donald P. Bellisario and Glen A. Larson.

In 1984, Selleck won an Emmy for Outstanding Lead Actor in a Dramatic Series, and in 1987, John Hillerman won an Emmy for Outstanding Supporting Actor in a Dramatic Series.

I've listed the season, episode, synopsis, writer, director, and guest stars for every show. Where I remembered an interesting anecdote or a bit of trivia, it's included. Also, if I referred to the episode earlier, I've referenced the chapter.

Episodes are numbered in sequence by season. The first episode of the first season is 1.1, the second episode of the first season is 1.2, and so on. All episodes are sixty minutes in length unless otherwise noted.

The cast of Magnum, P.I.

SEASON #1 (1980–81)

Episode 1.1—*Don't Eat the Snow in Hawaii* (2 hours, 12/11/80)

This two-hour pilot introduced the *Magnum* crew and found Thomas investigating the suspicious drug-related death of a wartime friend.

Written by Don Bellisario and Glen Larson; directed by Roger Young.

Guest stars included Pamela Susan Shoop, Allen Williams, Frank Kane, Eugenia Wright, Murray Salem, Fritz Weaver, W. K. Stratton, Robert Loggia, Jeff MacKay, Branscombe Richmond, Judge Reinhold.

This episode was partially filmed in Hollywood, particularly the club scenes at Rick's place—notice the set is different than any other episode. It was the first time I used a machine gun, and it set me up as a weapons expert.

Also, the episode was like a Baa Baa Black Sheep *reunion. Robert Loggia was the understudy director on* Black Sheep, *and W. K. Stratton and Jeff MacKay were two of my costars. Loggia returned to direct some* Magnum *episodes.*

Judge Reinhold, who had a small part in this episode, went on to star in the Beverly Hills Cop *movies. Allen Williams played reporter Adam Wilson on* Lou Grant.

Episode 1.2—*China Doll* (12/18/80)

Magnum is hired to guard beautiful Mai Lin and a valuable antique vase. Unbeknownst to Thomas is the true value of the artifact to a violent Chinese gang.

Written and directed by Don Bellisario.

Guest stars included Suesie Elena, Marvin Wong, George Cheung, Lee de Broux, and Yankie Chang.

I played a rickshaw driver and the villain was in the back with the vase. They shot this scene over twenty times, and I almost passed out from dehydration and exhaustion from pulling the rickshaw up and down the street.

Episode 1.3—*Thank Heaven for Little Girls and Big Ones, Too* (12/25/80)

Over the Christmas holiday, Magnum is hired by five school-girls to locate their "missing" teacher. Thomas boards the girls at the estate and a priceless painting disappears.

Written by Babs Greyhosky; directed by Bruce Seth Green.

Guest stars included Katherine Cannon, Lauri Hendler, Elizabeth Hoy, Shannon Brady, Al Harrington, and Jim Demarest.

During one scene, I was underwater. "Count to ten and then surface," ordered the director. Suddenly I saw this huge eel. To hell with counting to ten! At three, I leaped out and ruined the scene.

Katherine Cannon played the schoolteacher who married Merlin Olsen in the TV series Father Murphy.

Episode 1.4—*No Need to Know* (1/8/81)
The CIA enlists Magnum's help in protecting Higgins' former British commander from the IRA.

Written by Frank Lupo (who also created *The A-Team* with Stephen Cannell); directed by Larry Doheny.

Guest stars included Robin Dearden, Ed Grover, Richard Johnson, John Allen, Gene Hamilton, and Marika Van Kampen.

We celebrated Selleck's birthday during the filming of this episode. The cast bought him a bottle of Louis XIII for $1,100.

Episode 1.5—*Skin Deep* (1/15/81)
While investigating the apparent suicide of a gorgeous movie star, Magnum uncovers murder and is stalked by the killer.

Written by Don Bellisario; directed by Larry Doheny.

Guest stars included Ron Masak, Ian McShane, Cathie Shirriff, and Remi Abellira.

We dedicated this episode to Robert Vanderkar, the cameraman killed in a helicopter crash during production (see chapter 3).

Larry Doheny, the director, died on the set of a later Bellisario series, Tales of the Gold Monkey, *during preparation of an episode.*

Ron Masak played Sheriff Metzger on Murder, She Wrote.

Episode 1.6—*Never Again... Never Again* (1/22/81)
Magnum finds himself embroiled in a plot involving Nazis, holocaust survivors, Israeli intelligence, murders, and abduction.

Written by Babs Greyhosky; directed by Robert Loggia.

Guest stars included Hanna Hertelendy, Robert Ellenstein, Clay Wai, Earl Kingston, and Todd Camenson.

My role was expanded beginning with this episode.

Episode 1.7—*The Ugliest Dog in Hawaii* (1/29/81)
A wealthy woman hires Magnum to guard her small terrier, Algie, who is the target of dog-nappers.

Written by Don Bellisario, Frank Lupo, Chris Bunch, and Allan Cole; directed by Larry Doheny.

Guest stars included Paul Gale, Kathleen Nolan (past president of the Screen Actors Guild), Michael Gazzo, Michael Nader, and Shawn Hoskins.

The familiar Magnum *musical theme written by Mike Post was used for the first time in this episode. Mike went to high school with Selleck and has scored many popular TV series, including* The Rockford Files.

Episode 1.8—*Missing in Action* (2/5/81)

A singer with ESP at Rick's King Kamehameha Club asks Magnum to find her fiancé, a spy missing in action for eight years.

Written by Ken Pettus, Frank Lupo, and Craig Buck; directed by Robert Loggia.

Guest stars included Rebecca Holden, Lance LeGault, Francisco Lagueruela, and Jeff MacKay.

Rebecca Holden was a regular for one year in the series Knight Rider.

Episode 1.9—*Lest We Forget* (2/12/81)

Magnum searches for the former wife of a Supreme Court nominee thought dead at the time of Pearl Harbor.

Written by Don Bellisario; directed by Larry Doheny.

Guest stars included Anne Lockhart, June Lockhart, Miguel Ferrer, Jose Ferrer, Elizabeth Lindsey, and Scatman Crothers.

In an interesting bit of casting, Anne Lockhart and Miguel Ferrer played the same roles as their parents, June and Jose, in the flashback sequences. Miguel's mother is Rosemary Clooney. I became very friendly with Jose Ferrer and we played golf together while he was in Hawaii, even though I hate golf.

Scatman Crothers, who played Mingo in Roots, *was a great character actor who was a regular on* Chico and the Man, One of the Boys, *and other TV series and specials. He also did a number of lead voiceovers for cartoon series. Additionally, Scatman appeared in numerous movies, including* One Flew Over the Cuckoo's Nest, The Shining, *and* The King of Marvin Gardens.

Episode 1.10—*The Curse of the King Kamehameha Club* (2/19/81)

After an old Hawaiian places a curse on Rick's club, tragedy arrives and Magnum investigates.

Written by Babs Greyhosky; directed by Rick Kolbe.

Guest stars included Lew Ayres, Mann Tupou, Sol Bright, Cliff Coleman, and Gretchen Corbett.

My parents flew in from Chicago and surprised me while we were filming this episode. It was the first time they ever saw me working live in TV.

Of course, they were just as excited to see Ayres. They were great fans of his from his role as Dr. Kildare in the 1940s movies.

Gretchen Corbett is best known for her continuing role as Beth Davenport on The Rockford Files. *Several* Rockford Files *alumni appeared on* Magnum *over the years, including Noah Beery, Joe Santos, and Stuart Margolin.*

Episode 1.11—*Thicker Than Blood* (2/26/81)

T. C. smuggles a former Vietnam buddy who saved his life into Hawaii, unaware of his involvement in a huge drug caper.

Written by Don Bellisario; directed by Larry Doheny.

Guest stars included Vincent Caristi, Andre Philippe, Chip Lucia, Jeff MacKay, and Michael Spilotro (see chapter 6).

Director Larry Doheny, who worked on Baa Baa Black Sheep *with Bellisario and me, also taught Robert Loggia how to direct.*

Episode 1.12—*All Roads Lead to Floyd* (3/12/81)

A woman asks Magnum to find her missing father, unaware that he doesn't want to be found and that others are on his trail.

Written by Rogers Turrentine and Babs Greyhosky; directed by Ron Satlof.

Guest stars included Noah Beery, Anne Bloom, Red West, Andy Romano, and Georgia Schmidt.

Red West appeared with me on The Duke *as Sergeant O'Brien. I played a shady promoter named Joe Cadillac.*

Episode 1.13—*Adelaide* (3/19/81)

A prizewinning jumping horse named Norman is kidnapped, and Magnum is hired by the owner to investigate.

Written by Robert Hamilton; directed by Larry Doheny.

Guest stars included Cameron Mitchell and Christine Belford.

Cameron Mitchell befriended me and told me how he overcame a drinking problem. He also convinced me that the best way to stay healthy was to eat raw garlic. I started doing it until everyone on the set began avoiding me.

Episode 1.14—*Don't Say Goodbye* (3/26/81)

Hired to pay off a blackmailer by an old blind woman, Magnum is thrust into the middle of accidents, mayhem, and murder.

Written by Tim Maschler and Babs Greyhosky; directed by Rick Kolbe.

Guest stars included Andrea Marcovicci, Mercedes McCambridge, and Ted Danson.

Andrea is now a singer, and Ted went on to do Cheers. *He was a nice guy and we had a few dinners while he was in Hawaii. Danson and Selleck would later costar in the film* Three Men and a Baby *and the sequel,* Three Men and a Little Lady.

I've been a big fan of Mercedes McCambridge ever since I saw her shoot it out with Joan Crawford in the western Johnny Guitar. *She won an Oscar for* All the King's Men.

Magnum *gave us many opportunities to dress up and have fun.*

Episode 1.15—*The Black Orchid* (4/2/81)

Magnum is lured into participating in the fantasy dramas of 1930s detective thrillers by a rich eccentric woman, and a true-life mystery ensues.

Written by Robert Hamilton; directed by Ray Austin.

Guest stars included John Ireland, Judith Chapman, Robert Hoy, and Kathryn Leigh Scott.

This was one of my favorite episodes, and years later I named the restaurant Tom and I opened in Hawaii the Black Orchid (see chapter 4).

Director Ray Austin was part of the Bellisario-created-series family and later directed episodes of Airwolf, Quantum Leap, and JAG.

Episode 1.16—J. "Digger" Doyle (4/9/81)
Magnum and Higgins feel left out after Robin Masters hires a beautiful woman to beef up security at the estate to protect his latest novel. Later, Higgins is kidnapped and Magnum comes to the rescue.

Written by Don Bellisario; directed by Rick Kolbe.

Guest stars included Erin Gray, Stewart Moss, Bruce Atkinson, and Jacquelyn Ray.

This episode was intended as a spin-off for a new series starring Erin Gray of Buck Rogers *fame, but it never panned out. Later, she and I did a* Fantasy Island *episode together.*

Rick Kolbe was a director in Germany. He also directed some episodes of JAG.

Jackie Ray was Tom Selleck's ex-wife. In the final scene, she was supposed to drive up to me, stop, and then take off. I was wearing a great-looking outfit that I planned on "borrowing" from Wardrobe, but Jackie missed her mark, hit a mud puddle, and ruined "my" clothes.

Episode 1.17—Beauty Knows No Pain (4/16/81)
Broke and searching for her fiancé, fitness instructor Barbara Terranova offers to train Magnum for the Iron Man Competition if he'll find her man.

Written by Robert Hamilton; directed by Ray Austin.

Guest stars included Marcia Wallace, Jim Weston, Curtis Credel, and Louise Fitch.

The name Barbara Terranova was taken from the niece of Peter Terranova, then Vice President of Business Affairs for Universal.

Marcia Wallace played Carol, the receptionist on The Bob Newhart Show.

SEASON #2 (1981–82)

Episode 2.1—*Billy Joe Bob* (10/8/81)

A strong-willed Texas cowboy searching for his sister hires Magnum. It's shoot first—ask questions later, drugs, and prostitutes, as Billy Joe Bob tries to resurrect the Code of the West.

Written by Jeff Wilhelm; directed by Ray Austin.

Guest stars included James Whitmore Jr., Marla Pennington, Patrick Bishop, and Jimmy Borges.

This episode was a reunion for me, Tom, and Jimmy Whitmore Jr.—we worked together on The Rockford Files. *Jimmy and Tom also worked together in* The Gypsy Warriors *and* Boston and Kilbride.

One night Selleck and Whitmore picked me up for dinner in Tom's Jeep. It was pouring and I was wearing a linen suit. I sat in the back seat right in a puddle and proceeded to ride with the rain slanting into the back of the Jeep where I was sitting. I got soaked and had to throw away the suit. I think they must have done it on purpose.

Episode 2.2—*Dead Man's Channel* (10/15/81)

A marine biologist seeks Magnum's help in finding her missing father who disappeared while sailing in a "cursed" channel.

Written by Diane Frolov; directed by Ray Austin.

Guest stars included Wendy Girard, Ina Balin, Jeff MacKay, and Mamaluna.

Ina Balin was a great woman. She was a staunch supporter of third-world-country children. We first met in the early seventies. When we were costars on a two-hour Mannix *episode, she was very helpful to me, recognizing that I was a scared actor.*

Episode 2.3—*The Woman on the Beach* (10/22/81)

A mysterious woman appeals to Rick for help and then vanishes, leaving Rick to enlist Magnum to solve a thirty-five-year-old crime.

Written by Andrew Schneider; directed by Donald P. Bellisario.

Guest stars included Judith Chapman, Jack Hogan, Kenneth Mars, and Herman Wedemeyer.

This was the first time in my TV career that I had a closeup scene kissing a woman. We had to shoot the scene over and over again because I was smothering the woman and kissing her like we were in the back seat of a Chevy. Finally, Don Bellisario intervened and showed me how to do it in front of the camera. Afterwards he joked, "What's wrong with you? All Italians know how to kiss!"

Judith Chapman did a lot of daytime serials such as Days of Our Lives, As the World Turns, General Hospital, Ryan's Hope, *and* One Life to Live.

Jack Hogan was a casting director and ran an acting school. Kenneth Mars was in Blazing Saddles.

Episode 2.4—*From Moscow to Maui* (10/29/81)
Magnum and his buddies play romantics, assisting a Russian defector and his fiancée as they foil the KGB.

Written by Andrew Schneider; directed by Michael Vejar.

Guest stars included Jeffrey Pomerantz, Susan Heldfond, Allan Rich, Jan Ivan Dorin, and Marianne Muellerleile.

This show was shot on the North Shore and it was the first time I ever saw a monsoon. It rained so hard that the insurance kicked in because we went over budget due to the weather.

I also took tennis lessons whenever it wasn't raining.

This episode introduced Magnum as a former Navy Seal. At the time the Seals were basically unknown to the general public.

Episode 2.5—*Memories Are Forever* (11/5/81, 2 hours)
Magnum is shocked to discover his Vietnamese wife, long believed dead, is accompanying her present husband's delegation to discuss POW/MIA remains. Ordered back into the

Navy, Thomas, T. C., and Rick confront political intrigue, Vietnamese secret police, and revolutionaries.

Written by Don Bellisario; directed by Ray Austin.

Guest stars included Marta DuBois, Soon-Teck Oh, Clyde Kusatsu, Paul Burke, and Lance LeGault.

Marta DuBois is the wife of Sal Dano, who was Selleck's acting coach for years, and later became mine. Marta and Jeff MacKay were among the stars of Tales of the Gold Monkey.

Clyde Kusatsu was a regular on Tom's sitcom, The Closer.

Paul Burke was in lots of movies including The Thomas Crown Affair *and* Valley of the Dolls. *He also costarred in numerous TV series such as* Dynasty, Twelve O'Clock High, Naked City, *and* Santa Barbara.

Episode 2.6—*Tropical Madness* (11/12/81)
Magnum is mystified when a beautiful woman rebuffs him for Higgins. Complicating matters are a dwarf and a sumo wrestler.

Written by Robert Hamilton; directed by Larry Doheny.

Guest stars included Devon Ericson, Roy Dotrice, Jake Hoopai, and Bruce Johnson.

Episode 2.7—*Wave Goodbye* (11/19/81)
Police interfere with Magnum's investigation into the death of Kacy, a surfing pal.

Written by Reuben Leder; directed by Sidney Hayers.

Guest stars included Vic Morrow, W. K. Stratton, Wings Hauser, and John Calvin.

I was a big fan of Vic Morrow when he played in Combat. *Soon after this, he died in a film accident. Wings Hauser became a "B" movie star in films such as* L.A. Bounty, Frame Up, *and* Deadly Force, *to name a few.*

Sidney Hayers was a British director as was Ray Austin. Our series used a lot of British directors because they were very precise in what they wanted and insisted on good acting. This is due to the rigorous training that actors go through in England—not to say that American directors aren't good. It's just a different type of training with a different type of results.

Episode 2.8—*Mad Buck Gibson* (11/26/81)

Magnum tries to protect a novelist friend of Robin Masters' from self-destruction, back-alimony, and a nasty secret.

Written by Robert Hamilton; directed by Rick Kolbe.

Guest stars included Darren McGavin, Vera Miles, Wally Langford, and Jo Pruden.

Darren McGavin starred in the TV series Night Stalker. *During filming of this episode, I took him and his family to Sea World.*

Vera Miles reminisced about James Stewart, a favorite actor of mine.

Episode 2.9—*The Taking of Dick McWilliams* (12/3/81)

Magnum's old Navy buddy, who has become very wealthy, is kidnapped and his Japanese wife seeks Thomas's aid.

Written by Diane Frolov; directed by Rick Kolbe.

Guest stars included Guy Stockwell, Irene Yah-Ling Sun, and John Fujioka.

Guy Stockwell fit right in with our South Pacific theme since he costarred twenty years earlier in Adventures in Paradise.

Episode 2.10—*The Sixth Position* (12/17/81)

Acting as the bodyguard for world-renown ballet star, Kendall Chase, Magnum faces international intrigue and terror.

Written by Babs Greyhosky; directed by Sidney Hayers.

Guest stars included Andrea Marcovicci, Jeff MacKay, Signe Hasso, and Corinne Michaels.

Babs Greyhosky had been Don Bellisario's secretary in Dallas, Texas. Don gave her an opportunity to write episodes. She did a great job!

Episode 2.11—*Ghost Writer* (12/24/81)

A ghost writer for an eccentric inventor hires Magnum to protect her and her source material.

Written by Caroline Elias; directed by Ray Austin.

Guest stars included Patch MacKenzie, Elisha Cook, Louise Fitch, and Alan Fudge.

Elisha Cook appeared in a different role in this episode. Later, he became Ice Pick.

Episode 2.12—*The Jororo Kill* (1/7/82)

An assassin in Honolulu, stalking the prime minister of a small republic, is being tracked by reporter Kate Sullivan and Magnum.

Written by Alan Sutterfield, Reuben Leder, Andrew Schneider, and Don Bellisario; directed by Alan Levi.

Guest stars included Tyne Daly, Christopher Morley, Ed Fernandez, and Burr DeBenning.

This episode was aired several months before Tyne Daly debuted in Cagney and Lacey. *I had always loved her work after seeing her in* The Enforcer *with Clint Eastwood.*

Episode 2.13—*Computer Date* (1/14/82)

Hired to expose computer espionage and adultery by a wealthy industrialist, Magnum uncovers more than he bargained for—Rick as the alleged lover.

Written by Babs Greyhosky; directed by Robert Thompson.

Guest stars included Charles Aidman, Nancy DeCarl, and Jeff MacKay.

Nancy DeCarl is my wife. This was a terrific show and I was very proud of her (see chapter 6).

Episode 2.14—*Try to Remember* (1/28/82)

An accident in Robin's Ferrari leaves Magnum suffering from amnesia and the prime suspect in the death of a missing girl he was pursuing.

Written by Andrew Schneider and Reuben Leder; directed by Michael Vejar.

Guest stars included Nancy Grahn, Mark Withers, and Kwan Hi Lim.

Episode 2.15—*Italian Ice* (2/4/82)

Revenge and jealousy are a deadly combination after Magnum rescues the daughter of Robin Masters' friend in Italy.

Written by Don Bellisario; directed by Gilbert Shilton.

Guest stars included Mimi Rogers, Ann Dusenberry, Jean Claudio, and Lenny Montana.

Tom began dating Mimi Rogers and they later starred together in Divorce Wars. *In 1998, Mimi landed a prime role as Mrs. Robinson in* Lost in Space.

Episode 2.16—*One More Summer* (2/11/82)

Trying to protect a former Naval Academy teammate, Magnum joins a professional football team training in Hawaii.

Written by Reuben Leder and Del Reisman; directed by Rod Daniel.

Guest stars included David Wilson, Louise Sorel, Bill Edwards, Dick Butkus (see chapter 6), and Pat Morita.

Pat Morita was a very funny guy who lived in Hawaii. He was a stand-up comic who played in Happy Days *and, later, in* The Karate Kid.

Episode 2.17—*Texas Lighting* (2/18/82)

Magnum becomes the bodyguard of a female poker champ, and it's T. C. to the rescue when they become stranded on an island.

Written by Robert Hamilton; directed by Michael Vejar.

Guest stars included Julie Sommars, Jack Hogan, and Tony Brubaker.

Julie Sommars starred in The Governor and J. J. *(playing J. J.) and also appeared as Assistant D.A. Julie Marsh in* Matlock.

Episode 2.18—*Double Jeopardy* (2/25/82)

The estate serves as the locale for a movie version of one of Robin's books as Magnum tries to solve an accidental shooting.

Written by Babs Greyhosky and Reuben Leder; directed by Robert Totten.

Guest stars included Dana Wynter, Larry Pennell, Kathleen Nolan, Kwan Hi Lim, and Barry Nelson.

Larry Pennell was a friend of mine who looked exactly like Clark Gable.

Barry Nelson starred in two classic 1950s series, My Favorite Husband *and* The Hunter.

A classic beauty, Dana Wynter's acting career has spanned the last few decades. My favorite of her movies is Shake Hands with the Devil.

Episode 2.19—*The Last Page* (3/4/82)

A Vietnam vet jeopardizes Magnum's quest to reap vengeance against a former wartime foe, now a major drug dealer living in Honolulu.

Written by Andrew Schneider; directed by Alan Levi.

Guest stars included Robert F. Lyons, Kam Fong, Joanna Kerns, and Sonia Nilsen.

Robert F. Lyons was in Baa Baa Black Sheep, *and Joanna Kerns was in* Growing Pains *and Selleck's 1997–98 series,* The Closer.

Episode 2.20—*The Elmo Ziller Story* (3/25/82)

Higgins' half brother, Elmo, a Texas rodeo owner and total opposite of Higgins, involves Magnum in confusion and murder.

Written by Robert Hamilton; directed by Michael Vejar.

Guest stars included Robin Dearden, Barbara Rhoades, John Dennis Johnston, and Med Flory.

I played a rodeo clown and slipped and fell into horse manure. This was the first of numerous episodes involving Higgins and his half brothers.

Episode 2.21—*Three Minus Two* (4/1/82)
Magnum is hired to protect a business woman in the high-fashion industry after her partners begin to die.

Written by Robert Van Scoyk; directed by Sidney Hayers.

Guest stars included Jill St. John, Beverly Garland, Robert Harker, Denny Miller, and Don Lamond.

Beverly Garland had a long career in the movies and is also the owner of the Beverly Garland Hotel in Hollywood.

When Jill St. John walked out in her bikini, I fell off my chair.

SEASON #3 (1982–83)

Episode 3.1—*Did You See the Sun Rise?* (2 hours, 9/30/82)
A sabotage plot, engineered by a Russian agent who tortured Magnum in Vietnam, involves an unsuspecting T. C.

Written by Don Bellisario; directed by Ray Austin.

Guest stars included James Whitmore Jr., Jeff MacKay, Bo Svenson, Paul Burke, Lance LeGault, Jean Bruce Scott, and Marianne Bunch.

This was one of the best and most controversial episodes. In the end, Magnum shoots the Russian in cold blood. Many fans of the show tell me it was their favorite one (see chapter 11).

Bellisario's new series, Tales of the Gold Monkey, *premiered this season—the fall of 1982.*

Episode 3.2—*Ki'i's Don't Lie* (10/7/82)
A crossover episode with *Simon & Simon*, with mainland private investigators Rick and A. J. Simon (Gerald McRaney and Jameson Parker) coming to Hawaii to retrieve a stolen artifact that's included in a charity auction at Robin Masters' estate protected by Higgins and Magnum.

Written by Philip DeGuere and Bob Shayne; directed by Larry Doheny.

Guest stars included Morgan Fairchild, Gerald McRaney, Jameson Parker, and Liam Sullivan.

This crossover was done to help boost the sliding ratings of Simon & Simon. *The story concluded on* Simon & Simon, *in an episode titled "Emeralds Aren't a Girl's Best Friend." The episodes were re-edited so they could stand alone in syndication. After the crossover show,* Simon & Simon's *ratings began to climb, and the show went on for another couple years. Ironically, before* Magnum, *I was up for the part Jameson Parker played in* Simon & Simon.

Phil DeGuere was a former supervising producer of Baa Baa Black Sheep.

Episode 3.3—*The Eighth Part of the Village* (10/14/82)

While doing a favor for Higgins, Magnum finds a Japanese girl inside a crate and uncovers a bizarre case involving kidnapping, pearls, and mayhem.

Written by George Geiger; directed by James Frawley.

Guest stars included Kim Miyori, Richard Hill, Marilyn Tokuda, and Danny Kamekona.

Episode 3.4—*Past Tense* (10/21/82)

T. C. and Higgins are kidnapped in a chopper, which is used in a prison escape involving a criminal who was arrested by Magnum.

Written by Reuben Leder; directed by Michael O'Herlihy.

Guest stars included James Wainwright, Pat Studstill, Drew Snyder, and Jim Reynolds.

I had to dive off of a boat in a wet suit and was very nervous about it. As I asked Tom how I looked, he said, "Fine!" Then he pushed me in the water.

Episode 3.5—*Black on White* (10/28/82)

Rick and Magnum try to protect Higgins from African Mau Mau warriors out to exact revenge on ex-British soldiers.

Written by Don Bellisario; directed by Alan J. Levi.

Guest stars included Ian McShane, Lynne Moody, Gillian Dobb, and Glenn Cannon.

Episode 3.6—*Flashback* (11/4/82)
In a dream state, flip-flopping between present day and the 1930s, Magnum tries to solve a murder.

Written by Robert Hamilton; directed by Ivan Dixon.

Guest stars included Anne Lockhart, Rosemary Murphy, Robin Strand, and Lee Patterson.

This was one of numerous episodes directed by Ivan Dixon, the former costar of Hogan's Heroes. *Ivan began directing in the late 1960s and did* Nichols *with James Garner. He was among the first of the African-American TV directors, and in the early 1970s directed two feature films. He liked working in Hawaii so much, he moved there. Today he owns a radio station in Maui.*

Episode 3.7—*Foiled Again* (11/11/82)
Higgins is framed for murder during a fencing tournament and Magnum pursues the real killers.

Written by Rob Gilmer and Tom Greene; directed by Michael Vejar.

Guest stars included Dana Wynter, Paxton Whitehead, Patricia McCormack, and Robert Medeiros III.

Episode 3.8—*Mr. White Death* (11/18/82)
The motive is revenge as a former professional wrestler enlists the aid of Magnum and Higgins to track down his missing son.

Written by Reuben Leder and Rob Gilmer; directed by Jeff Hayden.

Guest stars included Ernest Borgnine (see chapter 6), James Edgcomb, Linda Ryan, and Reri Tava Jobe.

In one scene, Ernest Borgnine lifts me up over his head, spins me around, and tosses me. When I hit the ground, I fell on a sprinkler system, setting it off. So, I had to change clothes and do it again.

Borgnine told us about the filming of The Wild Bunch *and how he broke his ankle and had to do the entire film limping around in pain.*

Episode 3.9—*Mixed Doubles* (12/2/82)
Hired to protect an obnoxious tennis star, Magnum is perplexed when an old friend becomes the key suspect.

Written by Reuben Leder and Rob Gilmer; directed by Burt Kennedy.

Guest stars included Kim Richards, Claudette Nevins, and Henry Gibson.

I tried to learn how to play tennis because they couldn't use a stunt double. The director made me practice during all my free time, but it still didn't matter—I stunk!

Episode 3.10—*Almost Home* (12/9/82)
Pearl Harbor, forbidden love, and stolen government property are the ingredients leading Magnum to solve a decades-old court-martial.

Written by Rob Gilmer and Alan Cassidy; directed by Ivan Dixon.

Guest stars included Kathleen Lloyd, Jean Bruce Scott, Beulah Quo, Gilbert Green, and Stephen Elliott.

Episode 3.11—*Heal Thyself* (12/16/82)
Magnum comes to the aid of a former nurse in Vietnam. Now a hospital surgeon, she is the key suspect in the murder of three patients.

Written by Rob Gilmer; directed by Leo Penn.

Guest stars included Marcia Strassman, Ed Winter, Kario Salem, and Woody Eney.

Director Leo Penn, who passed away in 1998, was the father of Sean Penn. Ed Winter played Colonel Flag on M*A*S*H. *Marcia Strassman played Gabe Kaplan's wife on* Welcome Back, Kotter.

Episode 3.12—*Of Sound Mind* (1/6/83)
Magnum inherits over $50 million from a wealthy and despised practical joker, and becomes the prey of some upset relatives.

Written by Andrew Schneider; directed by Michael Vejar.

Guest stars included Roscoe Lee Browne, Donnelly Rhodes, Elaine Joyce, and James Murtaugh.

Roscoe Lee Browne won an Emmy for a guest appearance on The Cosby Show *in 1986. He's been in numerous movies and television shows. In the 1970s, he starred with Tony Curtis in* McCoy. *Donnelly Rhodes costarred in* Soap.

Episode 3.13—*The Arrow That Is Not Aimed* (1/27/83)
A samurai warrior must take his life if a valuable artifact is not recovered by Magnum.

Written by Steven Hensley, J. Miyoko Hensley, and Reuben Leder; directed by Jim Frawley.

Guest stars included Mako, Lee de Broux, Seth Sakai, and Tom Fujiwara.

Episode 3.14—*Basket Case* (2/3/83)
A young basketball star on Magnum's youth team is a troubled child victimized by her foster parents.

Written by Julie Friedgen; directed by Ivan Dixon.

Guest stars included Dana Hill, William Schallert, Jo Pruden, and Roy Apao Jr.

I had to play basketball in this episode and wasn't very good. Roger gave me lessons—but they didn't help.

Episode 3.15—*Birdman of Budapest* (2/10/83)
Magnum uncovers a KGB assassination plot while entertaining a woman claiming to be Robin Masters' former teacher.

Written by Louis F. Vipperman; directed by Michael Vejar.

Guest stars included Sylvia Sidney, Joseph Wiseman, Fritz Feld, and Jacquelyn Ray.

This was around the time I developed my love of birds, and I purchased a macaw and discussed it in a National Enquirer *article. As a result, people started sending me parrots as gifts.*

Tom's former wife, Jackie Ray, appeared as a guest star.

Episode 3.16—*I Do?* (2/17/83)

In order to go undercover while investigating theft in a family-owned business, Magnum marries the company president's niece.

Written by Rob Gilmer; directed by Ivan Dixon.

Guest stars included Katherine Cannon, Dick O'Neill, Nicolas Coster, and Mary Jackson.

Episode 3.17—*Forty Years from Sand Island* (2/24/83)

A forty-year-old murder is at the root of blackmail, politics, and a car accident involving Higgins.

Written by Rogers Turrentine, Rob Gilmer, and Reuben Leder; directed by Michael Vejar.

Guest stars included James Shigeta, Keye Luke, Marilyn Tokuda, and David Palmer.

*James Shigeta, the famous Japanese actor (*Die Hard, Flower Drum Song*), and I went to a sushi bar. He ordered clams. As the chef made dinner, he slapped a clam and it moved. "No way I'd eat that," I told James. So he took it from me and swallowed it.*

Episode 3.18—*Legacy from a Friend* (3/10/83)

Magnum investigates black-market operations and the death of his friend Marcus, a financially strapped lifeguard, who was seen driving an expensive car before drowning.

Written by Robert Hamilton; directed by Stuart Margolin.

Guest stars included Annie Potts, Rosemary Forsyth, Annette McCarthy, and St. John Smith.

Stuart Margolin played Angel on Rockford Files, *and throughout this episode I'd imitate Angel and "break" Stuart up. Annie Potts later starred in the sitcom* Designing Women.

Episode 3.19—*Two Birds of a Feather* (3/17/83)
Mysterious incidents surround a plane crash at the estate as Magnum and a Vietnam vet search for answers.

Written by Don Bellisario; directed by Virgil Vogel.

Guest stars included William Lucking, Richard Roundtree, Ann Doran, Chad Sheets, and Soon-Teck Oh.

This was the second Magnum *episode that served as a pilot for a spin-off series. Richard Roundtree and William Lucking would have starred in the series, but, like the first one (1.16), it didn't get picked up.*

Lucking played Colonel Lynch, the Fort Bragg prison commander who chased after The A-Team. *Interestingly,* Magnum, P. I. *recurring actor Lance LeGault followed him in* The A-Team *series as the pursuer. Roundtree, of course, starred in* Shaft.

Episode 3.20—*By Its Cover* (3/31/83)
A former Naval Academy pal involves Magnum in drug dealing and dueling government agencies.

Written by Rogers Turrentine, Rob Gilmer, and Don Bellisario; directed by Michael Vejar.

Guest stars included Stuart Margolin, Ronald Hunter, Carlene Watkins, and Ted Gehring.

Episode 3.21—*The Big Blow* (4/7/83)
During a lavish dinner party at the estate, a huge tropical storm forms the backdrop to an armed robbery, an attempt on Robin's life, and a childbirth.

Written by Reuben Leder; directed by Alan Levi.

Guest starts included Kelly Ward, Lori Lethin, Sondra Currie, Barry Van Dyke, and James Doohan.

We shot this episode indoors during the rainy season since we could not film outside. While nailing the window shut, I hit my finger and it hurt for weeks.

Sondra Currie is director Alan Levi's wife. James Doohan played Scotty ("beam me up") in the original Star Trek *series.*

Episode 3.22—*Faith and Begorrah* (4/28/83)
In search of a stolen sacred relic, another Higgins' half brother, Father Paddy MacGuiness, arrives in Hawaii.

Written by Don Bellisario; directed by Virgil Vogel.

Guest stars included Richard Johnson, Rebecca Kimble, Lee Canalito, and Terri Ann Linn.

Whenever Hillerman played these dual roles as his brothers from all over the world, most of us had little or no scenes. The plots revolved around the Higgins brothers.

SEASON #4 (1983–84)

Episode 4.1—*Home from the Sea* (9/29/83)
While out in the ocean on his surf-ski, Magnum capsizes and must remain afloat until rescued by Higgins, T. C., and Rick.

Written by Don Bellisario; directed by Harvey Laidman.

Guest stars included Susan Blanchard, R. J. Williams, Constance Forslund, and Robert Pine.

This was a very difficult episode for Tom since he had to tread water for most of the show. Naturally, I got seasick, and so did Harvey Laidman, the director. Harvey is now semi-retired. Most recently, he directed Andy Griffith's Matlock *television movies.*

Magnum wore a Rolex watch during this show and it helped enhance the popularity of Rolexes.

*This was the only episode that Bellisario wrote during this season, as he was busy with a new creation—*Airwolf, *starring Jan-Michael Vincent. Magnum semi-regulars Jean Bruce Scott and Lance LeGault costarred on* Airwolf.

Robert Pine starred in CHiPS.

Episode 4.2—*Luther Gillis: File #521* (10/6/83)
A search for a missing girl takes Magnum and St. Louis private eye Luther Gillis in opposite directions.

Written by Reuben Leder; directed by Virgil Vogel.

Guest stars included Eugene Roche, Melora Hardin, Gillian Dobb, and Kwan Hi Lim.

Eugene Roche's extensive TV credits include regular roles on Soap, Webster, *and* Perfect Strangers.

Episode 4.3—*Smaller than Life* (10/13/83)
A boyhood friend of Rick's enlists his aid in an insurance fraud caper.

Written by J. Rickley Dumm; directed by Alan J. Levi.

Guest stars included Cork Hubbert, Lenore Kasdorf, and Blackie Dammett.

I worked with a little person in this one after telling writer J. Rickley Dumm over dinner how much I wanted to work with little people—since I am fairly short myself.

In one scene I got stuck in a chimney with the little guy and had to go on a diet afterwards (see chapter 10).

Episode 4.4—*Distant Relative* (10/20/83)
Murder and mayhem occur when Magnum chaperones Rick's supposedly "innocent" sister around town.

Written by Nick Thiel; directed by Virgil Vogel.

Guest stars included Carol Channing, Elisha Cook, Alice Cadogan, and Kathleen Lloyd.

This was an outstanding show for which Tom won an Emmy award. I also did some of my best acting in this episode and I owe it to Virgil Vogel.

Virgil W. Vogel died in 1997. He never stopped directing. A gruff but beloved man, Virgil directed many westerns in the old days of Hollywood. He was Barbara Stanwyck's favorite director; he did her TV series, The Big Valley, *as well as a number of her feature films.*

Episode 4.5—*Limited Engagement* (11/3/83)
Magnum tries to save a retirement home while also investigating grocery store robberies.

Written by Richard Yalem and Jay Huguely; directed by Harvey Laidman.

Guest stars included Martha Scott and Mildred Natwick.

Episode 4.6—*Letter to a Duchess* (11/10/83)

Higgins rescues Lady Wilkerson, whom he had admired for years, only to find her more attracted to Magnum.

Written by Robert Hamilton; directed by Bernard Kowalski.

Guest stars included Jane Merrow, Max Kleven, and Terence Knapp.

Episode 4.7—*Squeeze Play* (11/17/83)

A high-stakes softball game between Magnum's team and a team of professionals could result in the loss of Robin's Nest estate.

Written by Reuben Leder; directed by Harry Falk.

Guest stars included Dick Shawn, Peter Isacksen, Debbie Zipp, and Eddie Deezen.

Similar to my efforts at tennis and basketball, I was not very good at softball. Selleck insisted that I practice on my time off, but I didn't. In one scene, Tom was so mad at me that between innings as we were running by each other, he shoved the softball real hard in my stomach and said, "Way to practice!"

A baseball fanatic, Reuben Leder always wrote sports or baseball trivia into his episodes.

Episode 4.8—*A Sense of Debt* (12/1/83)

In order to repay an old debt from Vietnam, T. C. climbs into the ring to complete a boxing tour for an injured fighter.

Written by Jay Huguely; directed by Ivan Dixon.

Guest stars included Denny Miller, Shannen Doherty, and Don Gibb.

Another sports episode. I played T. C.'s manager and we had to train for the match. Fortunately, I had experience boxing, so I made out okay in this episode.

This show took place in Detroit and featured Alan Tramel and Lou Whitaker of the Tigers.

Episode 4.9—*The Look* (12/8/83)
A former Saigon disc jockey needs Magnum's help with phone threats and the search for her former fiancé.

Written by Louis F. Vipperman; directed by Harry Falk.

Guest stars included Gretchen Corbett, Stephen Young, Ralph Strait, and Gillian Dobb.

I had to climb up to a crow's nest with binoculars, and the crew forgot about me for over an hour. Without a rope I couldn't get down by myself safely. As usual, I'm sure they did it on purpose.

Episode 4.10—*Operation: Silent Night* (12/15/83)
While flying Magnum, Higgins, and Rick to their Christmas rendevous, T. C.'s chopper breaks down on a deserted island about to be used for target practice by the Navy.

Written by Chris Abbott-Fish and Reuben Leder; directed by Michael Vejar.

Guest stars included Ed Lauter and Bruce French.

This was my favorite show because, for the most part, it only starred the four regulars (see chapter 7). Roger Mosley sang Up on the Roof *in this episode.*

Episode 4.11—*Jororo Farewell* (1/5/84)
On tour with his country's little league team, Prince Danny Lei of Jororo is protected by Magnum from terrorists.

Written by Reuben Leder; directed by Ivan Dixon.

Guest stars included Wesley Ogata, John Saxon, and Robert Ito.

Again, this episode was a baseball show written by Reuben Leder. The audience learned that Magnum's role model was Hall of Fame Baseball Star Al Kaline. I had never heard of him and thought they were referring to an alkaline battery.

Movie actor John Saxon was a karate expert and gave me some lessons during our time off.

Episode 4.12—*The Case of the Red-Faced Thespian* (1/19/84)

Accidentally hit on the head during a costume party at the estate, Higgins believes he is a Shakespearean actor. Complicating matters even more is a jewelry heist and murder.

The foxy lady with guest star Roscoe Lee Brown is me! They had to cut me out of my girdle.

Written by Robert Hamilton; directed by Ivan Dixon.

Guest stars included Ronald Lacey, June Chadwick, John McCook, Laurette Spang-McCook, and Colleen Camp.

I was dressed as Marie Antoinette, had a girdle on, and needed to relieve myself. There was a tiny bathroom and I got stuck in it with the dress over my head. I couldn't get my Levi's down either, so I started screaming, "Wardrobe!"

They broke open the door and had to cut me out of the girdle.

Episode 4.13—*No More Mr. Nice Guy* (1/26/84)

On his way to a Naval Academy class reunion, Magnum reluctantly agrees to help his friend Carol, now working with the district attorney, to expose police corruption.

Written by Nick Thiel; directed by Michael Vejar.

Guest stars included Kathleen Lloyd, James Emery, Sal Viscuso, and Jerry Harpin.

Episode 4.14—*Rembrandt's Girl* (2/2/84)

Magnum is hired by a bank teller and they are inadvertantly locked in the bank vault, where they discover counterfeit money.

Written by Chris Abbott-Fish; directed by James Frawley.

Guest stars included Carol Burnett, John McMartin, Deborah Pratt, and Jillie Mack.

Carol Burnett lived in Hawaii and was a great fan of the show. Jillie Mack was Selleck's girlfriend to whom he is now married.

Episode 4.15—*Paradise Blues* (2/9/84)

A former romantic flame of T. C.'s from Vietnam arrives in Hawaii one step ahead of drug dealers from Detroit out to kill her.

Written by Chris Abbott-Fish; directed by Bernard L. Kowalski.

Guest stars included singer Leslie Uggams, trumpeter Chuck Mangione, Nick Dimitri, and Wayne Van Horn.

The studio replaced the old Ferrari with a newer one and I bought the old one. When it was delivered to my house, the Ferrari wouldn't start, so I sold it three weeks later (see chapter 8).

Episode 4.16—*The Return of Luther Gillis* (2/16/84)

Magnum and St. Louis private eye, Luther Gillis, join forces once again to track down the kidnappers of Luther's girlfriend and Higgins.

Written by Reuben Leder; directed by John L. Moxey.

Guest stars included Sheree North, Geoffrey Lewis, Eugene Roche, Jeff Harlan, and Kanani Choy.

A great character actor, Geoffrey Lewis did numerous movies including a few with Clint Eastwood, including High Plains Drifter, Every Which Way but Loose, *and* Bronco Billy.

Episode 4.17—*Let the Punishment Fit the Crime* (2/23/84)

As Higgins is busy producing a Gilbert and Sullivan musical, Magnum busily searches for a missing brother, uncovers Chinese terrorists, and stops an assassination attempt.

Written by Robert Hamilton; directed by Bernard L. Kowalski.

Guest stars included Kay Lenz, Hermione Baddeley, Christopher Mitchum, Gillian Dobb, and Terence Knapp.

I had to take Japanese dance lessons and dress up as a geisha girl. When Selleck saw me, he couldn't stop laughing.

Episode 4.18—*Holmes Is Where the Heart Is* (3/8/84)

A former secret agent and old friend of Higgins arrives in Hawaii believing he is Sherlock Holmes and that Higgins is his sidekick, Dr. Watson.

Written by Judy Burns, Chris Abbott-Fish, and Jay Huguely; directed by John L. Moxey.

Guest stars included Patrick Macnee, Maurice Roeves, Michael Billington, George Kee Cheung, and Gillian Dobb.

We went to dinner with Pat Macnee (The Avengers), *and he told us stories about Sean Connery and his early career as a body builder before the James Bond movies.*

Episode 4.19—*On Face Value* (3/15/84)

Magnum injures a woman in a car chase while investigating a fencing operation for Deputy District Attorney Carol Baldwin.

Written by Nick Thiel; directed by Harvey Laidman.

Guest stars included Kathleen Lloyd, Talia Balsam, Tom Fujiwara, and Connie Kissinger.

Episode 4.20—*Dream a Little Dream* (3/29/84)

A surfer hires Magnum to protect her and her child during Hawaii's Surf-Out-Contest.

Written by Reuben Leder; directed by Roger E. Mosley.

Guest stars included Cindy Pickett, Alexander Diamond, Rosetta Tarantino, and Jeff Weston.

I was very impressed with Roger's effort at directing. Later, I went to the producers and said, "Roger directed an episode, how about me?" They gave me this strange look, so I walked away and never brought it up again.

Episode 4.21—*I Witness* (5/3/84)

Higgins, T. C., and Rick give conflicting accounts of a robbery at the King Kamehameha Club.

Written by Reuben Leder and Chris Abbott-Fish; directed by John L. Moxey.

Guest stars included Joy Garrett, Denise Nicholas-Hill, Ernest Harada, and Frank McRae.

I did a movie with Frank McRae in 1998 called Hijack.

This was a very funny episode and a fan favorite.

SEASON #5 (1984–85)

Episode 5.1—*Echoes of the Mind* (2 parts, 9/27/84 and 10/4/84)

Magnum is involved in the strange job of protecting a scared, emotionally scarred, beautiful society woman who believes someone is going to kill her.

Written by Donald P. Bellisario; directed by Georg Stanford Brown.

Guest stars included Sharon Stone, Carolyn Seymour, George Innes, Gillian Dobb, and Deborah Pratt.

Director Brown was married to Tyne Daly (Cagney & Lacey).

Sharon Stone (Basic Instinct, Casino) *played a dual role as twin sisters, and we knew it was only a matter of time until she hit it big.*

Episode 5.2—*Mac's Back* (10/11/84)

Magnum confuses fact and reality as he imagines his good friend, Mac, who was killed in a car explosion, is now alive as a Navy chaplain. As he follows the person he thinks is Mac, Magnum runs into an illegal gambling network.

Written by Donald Bellisario; directed by Alan Levi.

Guest stars included Jeff MacKay, Lance LeGault, Darryl Ferrera, and Glenn Cannon.

Jeff MacKay returned after doing Bellisario's other series, Tales of the Gold Monkey. *Jeff and Don were golfing partners.*

Episode 5.3—*The Legacy of Garwood Huddle* (10/18/84)

Magnum is in the unlikely position of helping an escaped bank robber find the loot from his last job so he can pay ransom to the kidnappers of the convict's young grandson.

Written by Rick Yalem; directed by Vincent McEveety.

Guest stars included Pat Hingle, John Ratzenberger, Belinda Montgomery, Elisha Cook, and Wakefield Mist.

Pat Hingle was a great character actor who, in the last few years, has played the police commissioner in the new Batman *movies. John Ratzenberger played mailman Cliff in* Cheers.

My wife, Nancy DeCarl, was visiting, and the show needed someone to play a newscaster. Since she had been one, Nancy was cast as a news reporter for this episode.

Episode 5.4—*Under World* (10/25/84)

T. C. is badly injured when he loses control of his helicopter and crashes into the ocean. Magnum tries to find out why the chopper went down and who is responsible.

Written by Reuben Leder; directed by Ivan Dixon.

Guest stars included Richard Lawson, Sam Vlahos, Rodney Aiu, James Grant Benton, and Michael Norton-Dennis.

Episode 5.5—*Fragments* (11/1/84)

After psychic Laura Griffin "sees" her own murder, she seeks Magnum's help to prevent the event, but her visions are really predicting events that will do Magnum in.

Written by Donald Bellisario, Nick Thiel, and David Chomosk; directed by David Hemmings.

Guest stars included Samantha Eggar, Kenneth Mars, Madeline Press, and Vic Leon.

A great actress and beauty, Samantha Eggar was unforgettable as the kidnapped woman in the 1965 film The Collector.

Episode 5.6—*Blind Justice* (11/8/84)

While helping Assistant District Attorney Carol Baldwin, Magnum finds evidence that clears a suspect of the murder he's charged with, but implicates him in another murder case for which he has avoided prosecution.

Written by Chris Abbott-Fish; directed by Russ Mayberry.

Guest stars included Kathleen Lloyd, Natalie Gregory, Barbara Rush, and George Dicenzo.

Episode 5.7—*Murder 101* (11/15/84)

While teaching a class for aspiring private investigators, Magnum gets involved in a real-life case as the fiancé of one of the students vanishes on his way to catch a plane.

Written by Rogers Turrentine; directed by Ivan Dixon.

Guest stars included Marilyn Jones, Alan Fudge, Frank Whiteman, Hunter Von Leer, and Kim Miyori.

Fans watching this episode didn't know it, but I had been hurt in an accident and was in a wheelchair. They never showed me in the chair, but it was a very challenging experience for the crew since I was driving my electric wheelchair around the set like a madman.

Episode 5.8—*Tran Quoc Jones* (11/29/84)

An Amerasian boy asks Magnum to locate his father, missing since the war in Vietnam. Magnum's efforts put him into conflict with gangsters and corrupt politicians.

Written by Chris Abbott-Fish; directed by Russ Mayberry.

Guest stars included Roland Harrah III, Rick Lenz, Terry Kiser, and Robert Tessier.

Rick Lenz costarred with Richard Boone in the early 1970s series Hec Ramsey.

Episode 5.9—*Luther Gillis: File #001* (12/6/84)

Blackmailers have evidence that could damage Higgins severely. Along comes tough St. Louis private investigator Luther Gillis, who hooks up with Magnum to identify the blackmailers and help Higgins.

Written by Reuben Leder; directed by Ivan Dixon.

Guest stars included Eugene Roche, Don Knight, and Gary Grubbs.

Episode 5.10—*Kiss of the Sabre* (12/13/84)

While on a forced leave of absence from the guest home by a novelist friend of Robin's, Magnum continues his work on an insurance case, but encounters the novelist who displaced him trying to solve the caper.

Written by Jay Huguely; directed by John Patterson.

Guest stars included Cassie Yates, Patrick Collins, Paul Gleason, Soon-Teck Oh, and David Spielberg.

Selleck played dual roles, Magnum and Sebastian Sabre, a Lance White-type character.

Cassie Yates played Judd Hirsch's wife in the short-lived series, Detective in the House, *which aired in the spring of 1985.*

Episode 5.11—*Little Games* (1/3/85)

It seems routine—hiring extra security during an exhibit of very valuable jewelry at Robin Masters' estate. But the security expert hired turns out to be the daughter of a notorious jewel thief who was thought to be retired.

Written by Deborah M. Pratt; directed by Arthur Seidelman.

Guest stars included Jenny Agutter, Cesar Romero, and Jo Pruden.

Every evening, Cesar Romero entertained us with stories of old Hollywood.

Episode 5.12—*Professor Jonathan Higgins* (1/10/85)

Magnum is on the case of Higgins' distant cousin Sally who arrives in Hawaii to get married. While investigating the intended groom, Magnum finds out some damaging facts that could change the wedding plans.

Written by Jay Huguely; directed by Peter Medak.

Guest stars included Jillie Mack, Lynn Wood, Ronald Knight, and Gillian Dobb.

Tom Selleck's girlfriend Jillie Mack played a trashy woman who became a lady. In a takeoff of My Fair Lady, *Higgins changed her.*

Episode 5.13—*Compulsion* (1/24/85)

Deputy District Attorney Carol is preparing to testify in a parole case involving a man whom her father had sent to prison, when strange and threatening events occur.

Written by Chris Abbott-Fish; directed by David Hemmings.

Guest stars included Kathleen Lloyd, John Pleshette, Gillian Dobb, and David Hemmings.

Episode 5.14—*All for One* (2 parts, 1/31/85 and 2/7/85)

Magnum, T. C., Rick, and Higgins are in Cambodia on the trail of an old friend being held prisoner by Vietnamese soldiers.

Written by Reuben Leder; directed by Michael Vejar.

Guest stars included Robert Forster, Clyde Kusatsu, Dustin Nguyen, Seth Sakai, and Nguyen Thinh Van.

Robert Forster starred in Banyon *(see chapter 2). He was recently nominated for an Academy Award for Best Supporting Actor in the 1997 feature film* Jackie Brown.

This was one of Magnum, P. I.*'s most expensive shows.*

Episode 5.15—*The-Love-for-Sale-Boat* (2/14/85)

Mac cons Rick by selling him a large luxury yacht he doesn't even own, along with four geisha girls. Before long everyone's life is in danger.

Written by J. Miyoko Hensley and Steven Hensley; directed by Ray Austin.

Guest stars included Jeff MacKay, Marilyn Tokuda, Elisha Cook, Nathan Jung, Kam Fong, Jeanne Kanai, and Masayo Ha.

Jeff MacKay and I had to do a scene eating sushi on the boat, stuffing our faces. We forgot that they had to reshoot each scene in closeup and other POV's (points of view). We must have eaten about twenty pounds of fish each and got sick as hell.

Rick's mentor Ice Pick was played by Elisha Cook Jr., a wonderful character actor. (My cuts and bruises were not real.)

Episode 5.16—*Let Me Hear the Music* (2/21/85)

Magnum is asked to help recover some very old love songs written for his nurse by a legendary country singer before he was killed in a plane crash twenty-five years ago.

Written by Jay Huguely; directed by David Hemmings.

Guest stars included Dennis Weaver, Rusty Weaver, Michael Cowell, Red West, Robby Weaver, and Susan Oliver.

TV star Dennis Weaver did his own singing and guitar playing in this episode. Rusty and Robby Weaver are his sons, and Rick Weaver, another son, was a Magnum, P.I. *producer.*

Red West, Elvis Presley's best friend and bodyguard wrote the book, Elvis—What Happened?

Episode 5.17—*Ms. Jones* (3/7/85)

Despite his misgivings about Mrs. Jones, Magnum agrees to help her find her husband, a computer expert who has discovered a valuable and dangerous formula.

Written by Phil Combest; directed by Ray Austin.

Guest stars included Margie Impert, Sam Anderson, Lance LeGault, Robert Hoy, and Marcia Wolf.

Episode 5.18—*The Man from Marseilles* (3/14/85)

Asked to locate a lost heir by a very famous European cop, Magnum's investigation leads to one of the world's biggest drug dealers.

Written by Reuben Leder; directed by John L. Moxley.

Guest stars included Kathleen Lloyd, Paul Verdier, Kwan Hi Lim, Elissa Dulce, and Edward Ruldolph.

Episode 5.19—*Torah, Torah, Torah* (3/28/85)

A valuable Torah is stolen, and Magnum and Rabbi Solomon work together to retrieve it amid danger and death.

Written by Sybil Adelman and Martin Sage; directed by Leo Penn.

Guest stars included France Nuyen, Arlen Dean Snyder, Nehemiah Persoff, and Peter Stader.

France Nuyen and Nehemiah Persoff were great movie actors. Persoff use to be in The Wild, Wild West, *and he and I exchanged stories about Bob Conrad.*

Episode 5.20—*A Pretty Good Dancing Chicken* (4/4/85)

It's Magnum in prison stripes on an undercover job at a prison farm. He needs to find out from a convict where he left his girlfriend who was seriously wounded during a stolen guns deal that went bad.

Written by Anthony Pellicano, Joe Gores, and Jay Huguely; directed by Bernie Kowalski.

Guest stars included Kathleen Lloyd, Asher Brauner, Matt Clark, Linda Grovenor, and Shannon Wilcox.

Writer Anthony Pellicano is one of the most famous detectives in the world. He was involved in the investigation of Michael Jackson on child molesting charges several years ago.

I grew up with Asher Brauner in Chicago, and he was in my first movie, Two Minute Warning.

SEASON #6 (1985–86)

Episode 6.1—*Déja Vû* (2 hours, 9/26/85)

Is it just a dream that Magnum is on his way to visit an old friend, or is it a coincidence when he arrives in London and finds out that the friend was hit by a black Jaguar and killed? As Magnum probes the mystery, he discovers his friend's troubling past.

Written by Donald Bellisario and Chris Abbott-Fish; directed by Russ Mayberry.

Guest stars included Peter Davison, Francesca Annis, Roy Stevens, and Pamela Salem.

Chris Abbott was a very good writer/producer who came up with a lot of great scripts with intricate twists. Her latest project was Dr. Quinn, Medicine Woman. *Russ Mayberry was an older director from the John Huston days.*

Tom wanted to stay at this very fancy hotel called Grosvenor House but they had banned actors, so he wasn't allowed.

Episode 6.2—*Old Acquaintance* (10/3/85)

Magnum is surprised when a high school friend visits him, and then gets involved with trying to rescue a kidnapped dolphin that has been trained to deliver a bomb strapped to its body to blow up a politician's yacht.

Written by Jill Sherman Donner; directed by Ivan Dixon.

Guest stars included Lee Purcell, Brock Peters, Keone Young, Lee de Broux, and Hari Rhodes.

Episode 6.3—*The Kona Winds* (10/10/85)

While on the beach, Magnum sees a woman about to drown in rough waters. He saves her, and they become attracted to each other, beginning a relationship that spells danger for Magnum.

Written by Chris Abbott-Fish; directed by Jay Jameson.

Guest stars included Cynthia Sikes, Frank Converse, Kit McDonough, and Dick Jensen.

Frank Converse was in Baa Baa Black Sheep *with me.*

Dick Jensen was a very famous Hawaiian entertainer, like Don Ho.

Episode 6.4—*The Hotel Dick* (10/17/85)

During preparations for a large convention of jewelry designers, Magnum is hired to capture a slippery cat burglar.

Written by Reuben Leder; directed by Doug Heyes.

Guest stars included Candy Clark, Granville Van Dusen, Wayne Storm, Phyllis Davis, and Norman Compton.

Norman Compton was Dolly Parton's bodyguard. Phyllis Davis began her continuing role as my girlfriend, Cleo. She also played Robert Urich's secretary in the series Vega$. *We shot this entire show in a hotel.*

Episode 6.5—*Round and Around* (10/24/85)

While investigating the murder of T. C.'s friend during a local convenience store robbery, Magnum finds the circumstances unsettling.

Written and directed by Reuben Leder.

Guest stars included Sheila Frazier, Grant Hubley, Rummel Mor, Larry B. Scott, and Bob Minor.

Bob Minor was a stunt coordinator who was also Roger Mosley's double.

Episode 6.6—*Going Home* (10/31/85)
Magnum returns home to attend his grandmother's funeral and gets involved with all sorts of unresolved personal relationships from his past.

Written by Don Balluck; directed by Harry Harris.

Guest stars included Gwen Verdon, David Huddleston, Joe Regalbuto, and Julie Cobb.

Joe Regalbuto was in the movie Lassiter *with Selleck, but he's more famous for his continuing role of Frank in* Murphy Brown.

We filmed a scene at the newly finished Vietnam Memorial Wall in Washington, D.C.

Episode 6.7—*Paniolo* (11/7/85)
On the trail of cattle thieves in Hawaii, Magnum teams up with his friends to track and capture a notorious rustler.

Written by Jay Huguely; directed by Russ Mayberry.

Guest stars included Henry Darrow, Michael Sharrett, Mary Kate McGeehan, Doug McClure, and Kawika Pagan.

We shot this episode on the Parker Ranch, the biggest ranch in Hawaii, and included scenes from the mountains where it snows. Selleck's personal horse was shipped over from L.A. This was my first time on horseback and my first time in a western, and I loved it.

Doug McClure had a great movie and TV career, especially in westerns. He and James Drury were the only two cast members of the television series The Virginian *who remained in the series the entire ten years. Toward the end, the series was renamed* The Men from Shiloh. *Lee Majors joined the cast for the last year.*

Episode 6.8—*The Treasure Of Kalaniopu'u* (11/11/85)
A publishing company has hidden one million dollars somewhere on an island as a publicity stunt. Hired to oversee the treasure hunt, Magnum is convinced that someone is prepared to kill for the money.

Written by Reuben Leder; directed by Ivan Dixon.

Guest stars included Kathleen Lloyd, Nancy Stafford, Beverly Todd, Kwan Hi Lim, and Glenn Carson.

We jumped off a cliff into a freshwater lake, upsetting the studio because we were supposed to use stunt doubles.

Episode 6.9—*Blood and Honor* (12/5/85)

Magnum goes on the trail of several suspects who could be leaking information contained in a manual for a top-secret nuclear submarine.

Written by Phil Combest; directed by Michael Vejar.

Guest stars included Paul Burke, Jeff Yagher, Simone Griffeth, Dennis Haysbert, and Chris Mulkey.

Director Vejar was an excellent athelete. He was all business as a director.

Episode 6.10—*Rapture* (12/12/85)

Magnum has a recurring vision of a young boy scuba diving without any breathing gear. Following an investigation, Magnum learns of the terrible tragedy that claimed the boy's life.

Written by Bruce Cervi; directed by Russ Mayberry.

Guest stars included Haunani Minn, John Bennett Perry, Eddie Barth, Robby Weaver, Josie Over, and Kahale Ahina.

Robby Weaver, one of Dennis Weaver's sons, played a newspaper reporter, and I was able to visit the Honolulu Advertiser *to see how a newspaper actually operated.*

Episode 6.11—*I Never Wanted to Go to France, Anyway* (1/2/86)

Magnum investigates unusual accidents at a traveling carnival visting Hawaii.

Written by Reuben Leder; directed by Arthur Seidelman.

Guest stars included Anne Scheedeen, Geoffrey Lewis, Clive Revill, Tommy Madden, and Anne Willmarth.

In the plot, we went undercover as carnival roustabouts in order to catch the villain. It was set at a real carnival and I went into the House of Mirrors and couldn't find my way out for forty-five minutes.

Episode 6.12—*Summer School* (1/9/86)

Thomas's life is in danger after Robin's nephew impersonates Magnum. The Ferrari is riddled with bullets by union thugs mistaking Magnum as an investigator of union racketeering.

Written by Bruce Cervi; directed by Russ Mayberry.

Guest stars included Meredith MacRae, Duff King, Russ McCubbin, and Michael MacRae.

Writer Bruce Cervi was the brother-in-law of Robert Harris when he was President of Universal.

Meredith MacRae was the daughter of Broadway and movie musical stars Gordon and Shirley MacRae. Every time I walked by Meredith, I sang a tune from Oklahoma.

Episode 6.13—*Mad Dogs and Englishmen* (1/23/86)

After Higgins' surprise departure from his job, rumors abound that Higgins had stolen money and valuable art objects. Magnum's investigation uncovers a frame-up and corrupt politicians.

Written by Jay Huguely; directed by Virgil Vogel.

Guest stars included Darleen Carr, Jeff Olson, Gillian Dobb, and Michael Halsey.

Darleen Carr was married to Jameson Parker of Simon & Simon. *He got the role I was up for before* Magnum.

Episode 6.14—*All Thieves on Deck* (1/30/86)

A priceless wooden Hawaiian statuette being given by Robin to the Hilo Museum is stolen, and Magnum must catch the thief on a cruise ship.

Written by Reuben Leder; directed by Jerry Jameson.

Guest stars included William Windom, Sarah Douglas, Alan Hale Jr., and Paul Sand.

We rented a big cruise ship that included paying customers, too, and I took my wife, Nancy, and son, Lorenzo, along. The guest star was Alan Hale, who had played the skipper on Gilligan's Island. *I had first met him in 1972, shortly after I arrived in Los Angeles, when he owned Alan Hale's Lobster House on LaCienega Boulevard. I was in awe of Alan and I had also seen every film that his father, Alan Hale Sr., had made. He told me all about his dad's cronies, John Barrymore and Errol Flynn.*

From the beginning of the episode, the weather was bad, and the entire shoot was problematic. I hated boats and I hated water, and I was sick as a dog because I couldn't find my "legs." At night, since there was nothing to do and the weather halted the shooting, everyone hung out in the bar on the boat, the only familiar and comfortable place for me. Ordinarily we shot each episode in about eight to ten days max. This one turned into a two-week shoot. It was like the show from hell.

William Windom won an Emmy for My World and Welcome to It. *He also played Dr. Seth Haslett in* Murder, She Wrote. *Additionally, Windom starred in* The Farmer's Daughter, *which ran on ABC from 1963 to 1966 and occasionally costarred my wife, Nancy, as the girlfriend of Windom's son.*

Episode 6.15—*This Island Isn't Big Enough* (2/13/86)

Rick and his guest are presumed dead when they do not return from a cruise at sea. Magnum, T. C., and Higgins set off in a race to locate Rick, mobsters, and two million dollars in counterfeit money.

Written by Chris Abbott-Fish and Reuben Leder; directed by Leo Penn.

Guest stars included Kathleen Lloyd, Clyde Kusatsu, and Jenny Sherman.

I only had one scene is this episode so I took off for L.A. and couldn't be found for ten days.

Episode 6.16—*Way of the Stalking Horse* (2/20/86)
Violence claims Magnum as he searches for a missing father.
Despite his wounds, he goes after the gunman while also try-
ing to save a young girl's life.

Written by Bruce Cervi; directed by John L. Moxey.

Guest stars included Kathleen Lloyd, Morgan Stevens,
Marta Kober, and Elisha Cook.

Aside from costarring with Bogart in The Maltese Falcon,
Elisha Cook considered his recurring role in Magnum, P. I. *the*
highlight of his life. Toward the end of his long career he struggled
with his lines, but he was still a class act.

Episode 6.17—*Find Me a Rainbow* (3/13/86)
While a group of underprivileged boys are enjoying Robin's
estate, one turns up missing. Magnum uncovers a black-market
baby ring and finds the missing boy.

Written by Jill Sherman Donner; directed by Rick Weaver.

Guest stars included Julie Montgomery, Kenneth David
Gilman, and Jennifer Salt.

Episode 6.18—*Who Is Don Luis Higgins... and Why Is He*
Doing These Terrible Things to Me? (3/20/86)
The president of Costa De Rosa is attending a chess tournament, and Magnum is asked to apprehend the person who has
been threatening to kill the president. The main suspect is
another half brother of Higgins named Don Luis.

Written by Jay Huguely; directed by John L. Moxey.

Guest stars included Robert Hogan, Cesare Danova, and
Anthony LaPaglia.

Episode 6.19—*A Little Bit of Luck... A Little Bit of Grief*
(4/3/86)
Magnum and T. C. attempt to retrieve a one million dollar
prize Rick won on a TV show that was later stolen in a fake-
kidnapping scam.

Written by Reuben Leder; directed by Ray Austin.

Guest stars included Claudia Cron and Pat Corley.

Director Ray Austin began his career in England as a stunt coordinator and second unit director. He ate oranges all day and every night we could always find him at the sushi bar.

Episode 6.20—*Photo Play* (4/10/86)

After Magnum's car is hit by a photographer's car, she enlists his help in apprehending embezzlers and murderers who appear in some newly developed old film.

Written by Charles Floyd Johnson and Bruce Cervi; directed by Burt Brinckerhoff.

Guest stars included Gillian Dobb and Cassie Yates.

Gillian Dobb, who played the recurring role of Agatha Chumbley, was a consummate actress who lived in Hawaii.

Director Brinckerhoff continues to direct TV series such as Promised Land *and* Touched by an Angel.

SEASON #7 (1986–87)

Episode 7.1—*L.A.* (2 hours, 10/1/86)

In this two-hour episode set in Los Angeles, Magnum has encounters with two women. First, a stand-up comic he meets is found dead in his hotel room. Later, during the murder investigation, Magnum proposes to an attorney, Cynthia Farrell, to whom he had served papers at the behest of Robin Masters.

Written by Chris Abbott-Fish; directed by Alan Levi.

Guest stars included Dana Delany, Mona Miller, Daniel Faraldo, Paul Grayber, Ina Balin, Alfonso Ribeiro, Kwan Hi Lim, and Michael Goodwin.

At the beginning of this season, Tom began co-producing the show and was very involved in casting, editing, and other facets of production.

Dana Delany went on to star in China Beach.

Episode 7.2—*One Picture Is Worth...* (10/8/86)

A deaf woman witnesses a bank robbery in which four people are killed. Fearing for her life after she identifies one of the killers, she turns to Magnum for help.

Written by James Novack; directed by Ray Austin.

Guest stars included Kathleen Lloyd, Stephanie Dunnam, and Tim Rossovich.

Rossovich was a high school classmate of Tom's, and also a great football player.

Episode 7.3—*Straight and Narrow* (10/15/86)

Magnum is hired by a former prostitute he knew years ago. Her sister has been involved with well-known politicians and is missing.

Written by Reuben Leder; directed by Harry Harris.

Guest stars included Candy Clark, Cindy Fisher, Jonathan Goldsmith, and George McDaniel.

Cindy Fisher starred opposite Matt Dillon in the 1981 movie Liar's Moon. *Candy Clark is best known for her role in* American Graffitti.

Episode 7.4—*A.A.P.I.* (10/22/86)

While presenting Magnum with the Local P.I. of the Year Award, a famous French detective suddenly drops dead. Magnum pursues his murderer and becomes entangled with drug smugglers.

Written by Reuben Leder; directed by Alan Levi.

Guest stars included Kathleen Lloyd, Paul Verdier, Annie Potts, Brian Clark, and Stephen J. Cannell.

We used a look-alike talent agency to help cast this episode—in the audience at the private detective convention were Columbo, Mike Stone (Karl Malden), and Kojak.

Everyone wanted James Garner to do a cameo as James Rockford but he was in the middle of his lawsuit against Universal and refused to walk onto one of their sets. Eventually he settled the case and was rumored to have received millions.

Stephen J. Cannell, who guest starred, was a producer and writer for Baa Baa Black Sheep, Rockford Files, The A-Team, and Renegade. *He has also written three novels.*

Episode 7.5—*Death and Taxes* (10/29/86)
Mayhem dogs Magnum at the estate while Higgins is away at the annual writers' conference. Known as the Ripper, a caller obsessed with Magnum's old cases taunts him with riddles predicting death.

Written by Bruce Cervi; directed by Alan Levi (see chapter 7).

Guest stars included Ken Tigar, Jean Bruce Scott, Gary Frank, and Joe Santos.

Joe Santos had a recurring character on The Rockford Files. *Ken Tigar played the role of Heath in the final season of* Dynasty.

Episode 7.6—*Little Girl Who* (11/5/86)
Magnum helps his ex-wife, Michelle, and her five-year-old daughter escape from murderous Vietnamese soldiers to reach freedom and safety.

Written by Deborah M. Pratt; directed by Ray Austin.

Guest stars included Marta DuBois, Kristen Carreira, Soon-Teck Oh, and Lloyd Kino.

There was a gunfight between Magnum and a Vietnamese villain in the street, and it appeared to me that Tom got hit with a projectile from the gun. I freaked and ran out to where Tom was lying to see if he was all right. He was fine, but the scene was ruined, and the director screamed at me for the rest of the week.

Episode 7.7—*Paper War* (11/12/86)
Squabbles erupt between Magnum and Higgins over his memoirs while Magnum is involved with a notorious group running a gambling ring.

Written by Jay Huguely; directed by Tony Wharmby.
Guest stars included James Shigeta and Richard Narita.
I had a lot of fun during this episode because it was a show with a lot of practical jokes. The writers knew that we played jokes on each other all the time and so they followed that theme.

Episode 7.8—*Novel Connection* (11/19/86)
Someone wants one of Robin Masters' guests dead, and Magnum works with mystery writer Jessica Fletcher, from the mainland, to keep everyone alive and uncover the killer.
Written by Jay Huguely; directed by Harry Harris.
Guest stars included Angela Lansbury, Dorothy Loudon, Jessica Walter, Ramon Bieri, and Stephanie Faracy.
This was a crossover episode with Murder, She Wrote. *The story continued in an episode of* Murder, She Wrote *called "Magnum on Ice" (11/23/86).*

Angela Lansbury wore a watch with an alarm and when it went off, she'd quit working for the day. It didn't matter if it was in the middle of a scene or whatever—she was finished! The cast and crew weren't thrilled about that.

Episode 7.9—*Kapu* (11/26/86)
A Hawaiian girl witnesses a mob killing and Magnum is wounded while trying to protect her. Knocked out, he wakes up on a forbidden island hunted by the killers.
Written by Deborah Dean Davis; directed by Ivan Dixon.
Guest stars included Elisha Cook, Larry Pennell, Marlene Sai, Deborah Calbero, and Dick Jensen.

Episode 7.10—*Missing Melody* (12/3/86)
After T. C.'s children, Melody and Bryant, come to visit, Melody is kidnapped and a ransom note arrives asking for $300,000. Magnum suspects that the cousin of T. C.'s ex-wife is involved in the kidnapping.

Written by Roger E. Mosley and Cal Wilson; directed by Harvey Laidman.

Guest stars included Fay Hauser, Shavar Ross, Martina Stringer, Lillian Lehman, Tom McFadden, Alfonso Riberio, and Albert Popwell.

T. C.'s estranged family is introduced in Roger's first foray into television writing.

Episode 7.11—*Mentor* (12/10/86)

Magnum and Carol are concerned when her mentor—a judge—starts behaving strangely. Confronted with evidence of corruption, he is later found dead. Meanwhile, Rick's mentor, Ice Pick, is also involved with the judge's criminal cronies.

Written by Maryanne Kasica and Michael Scheff; directed by Jerry Jameson.

Guest stars included Kathleen Lloyd, Michael Constantine, Elisha Cook, Pat Li, Kwan Hi Lim, and William Watson.

This episode contained flashbacks of my character's past and revealed how Ice Pick became my surrogate father.

Michael Constantine won an Emmy in 1970 for Best Supporting Actor in a Comedy for his role in Room 222.

Episode 7.12—*Autumn Warrior* (12/17/86)

Higgins takes a group of boys from a prison farm to an island for survival training. While there, the convicts mutiny and Magnum and T. C. intercede.

Written by Jay Huguely; directed by Tony Wharmby.

Guest stars included Warren Fabro, Reginald T. Dorsey, Peter Kowanko, and Dennis Haskins.

Episode 7.13—*Murder by Night* (1/14/87)

It's TV noir, as the cast is involved in a murder case set in the 1940s, and Magnum is surrounded by characters who look familiar. Filmed in black and white, the screen returns to color as Magnum solves the case.

Written by Robert Hamilton; directed by Russ Mayberry.

Guest stars included Anne Twomley, Phyllis Davis, and Jennifer Runyon.

This was a takeoff on the Humphrey Bogart movies, and I played the Peter Lorre character from The Maltese Falcon.

Episode 7.14—*On the Fly* (1/21/87)
A Mexican mob boss pursues Magnum in a case of mistaken identity that leads to T. C. being shot and Mac injured.

Written by Jay Huguely; directed by Bernie Kowalski.

Guest stars included Jeff MacKay, Annette Cardona, Mike Moroff, and Bryne Piven.

I used to work with Bryne Piven on the series, The Duke, *with Robert Conrad.*

Episode 7.15—*Solo Flight* (2/4/87)
Fired from a case, Magnum seeks solace in the mountains only to become trapped under the wreckage of a World War II airplane, where he is forced to re-examine his values and face his mortality.

Written by Jay Huguely; directed by John Flinn III.

Guest stars included Norman Fell.

Director Flinn was a high school classmate of Selleck's. He was always kidding around with the crew but detested vulgarity on the set.

Norman Fell played landlord Stanley Roper on Three's Company.

Episode 7.16—*Forty* (2/11/87)
While investigating arms dealing, Magnum falls for a beautiful TV newscaster who uses him to complete her investigative report. He returns home to a surprise fortieth birthday party.

Written by Bruce Cervi; directed by Russ Mayberry.

Guest stars included Gwen Verdon, Patricia Martinez, and James Luisi.

James Luisi was a regular on The Rockford Files *and was also in an episode of* The Streets of San Francisco *with me.*

Episode 7.17—*Laura* (2/25/87)

Magnum helps a retired New York City policeman locate the killers of his granddaughter.

Written by Chris Abbott-Fish; directed by Alan Levi.

Guest stars included Frank Sinatra, Kevyn Major Howard, Joe Santos, Jack Kruschen, and Kristin Brick.

Laura, *the episode title, is also the name of Sinatra's favorite song (see chapters 6 and 7).*

Character actor Jack Kruschen was my neighbor in Hawaii.

Episode 7.18—*Out of Sync* (3/11/87)

Magnum's fiancée Cynthia (from the L.A. episode) visits Hawaii for the weekend, but their time is interrupted by an actress in porn movies who believes her boyfriend is making snuff films.

Written by Jay Huguely; directed by Joan Darling.

Guest stars included Dana Delany, Lisa Blount, and David Hemmings.

Episode 7.19—*The Aunt Who Came to Dinner* (3/18/87)

Magnum's aging Aunt Phoebe, a famous playwright, arrives in Hawaii convinced that someone is trying to kill her.

Written by Chris Abbott-Fish; directed by Russ Mayberry.

Guest stars included Barbara Rush, Mark Stevens, Katherine Kelly Lang, and Fred Sadoff.

A superb actress, Barbara Rush worked in movies with some of the great ones: Paul Newman (Hombre, The Young Philadel-

SHOOTING CALL SHEET — UNIVERSAL CITY STUDIOS — MAGNUM P.I.

GENERAL CALL 12:30 P — SHOOTING CALL 1:15 P — SHOOTING DAY NO. 1 — DATE Monday 1-5-87

PICTURE "LAURA" — PROD. NO. 61927 — DIRECTOR ALAN LEVI

PAGES	SET DESCRIPTION	SC. NO.	D/N	LOCATION
4 6/8	Int. Jail Cell (Magnum, Doheny, Rick, Page, Atmos)	45	D	Stage
	— Company Move —			
3	Ext. International Market Place (Magnum, Doheny, Geiger, Clayton, Woman Biker, N.D. Woman, Dbls, Atmos.)	80 thru 105	N	Int'l Market Place

CAST	CHARACTER	CALL TIME	REMARKS	SET CALL
1. TOM SELLECK	MAGNUM	12:45 PM	RPT. STUDIO	
2.				
3.				
4. LARRY MANETTI	RICK	12:15 PM	P.U. @ HOME	
5. FRANK SINATRA	DOHENY	12:30 PM	P.U. @ Colony	
8. KEVYN MAJOR HOWARD	GEIGER	5 PM	P.U. @ COLONY	
9. STEVEN KEATS	CLAYTON	5 PM	P.U. @ COLONY	
10. JOE SANTOS	LT. PAGE	12:30 PM	P.U. @ COLONY	
15. ALLEN MICHAEL LERNER	MURRAY	TRVL FROM L.A.		
KATHY BECK (Now)	BIKER (F)	6:30 PM	RPT TO STUDIO	
MEG ROACH (Now)	LADY IN MACESTRENE (F)	6:30 PM	RPT TO STUDIO	
LOREN JANES ST DBL DOHENY		12:30 PM	P.U. @ COLONY	
BOB MINOR STUNT COORDINATOR		6:30 PM	STUDIO TOM LUPO UTILITY STUNT NEW 6:30 PM RPT STUDIO	

ATMOSPHERE	CALL TIME	REMARKS
standins: J. NORDLUM 12:30 PM Tom Richaros 12:30 PM Lv studio 12:30 PM J. THOMPSON, J. CUTRER 12:30 PM		
12:30 PM 1 UNIFORMED POLICEMAN	RPT. TO STUDIO	
6:30 PM 60 MARKET PLACE ATMOS —	RPT TO STUDIO	

ADVANCE: Int. Stairwell — (Laura) — SC. 12
Ext. Kalakaua Towers (Mag, Doheny, Murray) — 51 THRU 57
Int. Kalakaua Towers (Mag, Doheny, Murray) — 48, 49, 50
Int. Deserted Bldg. (Doheny, Dbls) — 130,134,155
Ext. Rooftop (Mag, Rick, Doheny, Geiger, Page, Dbls) — 146 THRU 153

2ND A.D'S: S. BURNAM / B.WILLIAMS
PROD.MGRS: MARK SCHILZ/WARREN SMITH — 1ST ASST. DOUG WISE — INTERN P.SCHMETZER

A piece of TV history: the call sheet for the Frank Sinatra episode, "Laura."

phians), *Marlon Brando* (The Young Lions), *Frank Sinatra* (Come Blow Your Horn, Robin and the Seven Hoods), *and Kirk Douglas* (Strangers When We Meet).

Episode 7.20—*The People vs. Orville Wright* (4/1/87)
Magnum gets involved on Rick's behalf after Rick is arrested for murdering a hit man who had been contracted to murder his mentor, Ice Pick.

Written by Bruce Cervi; directed by Burt Brinckerhoff.

Guest stars included Elisha Cook, Lyman Ward, Kathleen Lloyd, and Kwan Hi Lim.

Kwan Hi Lim, who played Lieutenant Tamaka, was a very funny guy, a latter-day Charlie Chan.

Episode 7.21—*Limbo* (4/15/87)
Wounded in a shootout, Magnum falls into a coma and lingers between life and death. In this comatose-state, he finds his ex-wife and helps her escape from killers.

Written by Tom Selleck, Jay Huguely, Bruce Cervi, and Chris Abbott-Fish; directed by Jackie Cooper.

Guest stars included Kathleen Lloyd, Jeff MacKay, Jean Bruce Scott, Marta DuBois, Kristen Carreira, Lance LeGault, John Beck, and Kwan Hi Lim.

A very bizarre show; Magnum is ghost-like and we had to act like he wasn't.

Lance LeGault began entertaining as a singer. Like me, he loved fast cars.

Originally, this was to be our last Magnum, P. I. *episode, but at the last moment, we all signed on for one more season, albeit a short one. Therefore, the script, which called for Magnum to die, was changed.*

SEASON #8 (1987–88)

Episode 8.1—*Infinity and Jelly Doughnuts* (10/7/87)
Picking up where the final episode of season #7 ended, Magnum comes out of the coma but is still in critical condition.

Written by Chris Abbott-Fish; directed by John C. Flinn, III.

Guest stars included Kathleen Lloyd, Jeff MacKay, Jean Bruce Scott, Gwen Verdon, John DiAquino, and Richard Narita.

Selleck's parents and his adopted son Kevin made guest appearances in this episode.

Gwen Verdon played Magnum's mom. I'm sure Tom had a lot to do with casting her because she had many of the great qualities Selleck's real mother possessed.

Episode 8.2—*Pleasure Principle* (10/14/87)

When Higgins takes a vacation, leaving Magnum in charge of the estate, they each undergo personality changes—Higgins becomes looser while Magnum becomes a stuffed shirt.

Written by Jay Huguely; directed by Corey Allen.

Guest stars included Julia Migenes, Gregory Sierra, Amy Yasbeck, Gillian Dobb, and Jeff MacKay.

Director Corey Allen was the actor in Rebel without a Cause *who raced the car against James Dean. His dad worked in Las Vegas and gained notoriety for punching Sinatra when Frank drove his golf cart through the window of the Sands Hotel.*

Episode 8.3—*Innocence...A Broad* (10/28/87)

While helping Higgins expose the illegal activities of a mob character, Magnum is assisted by a browbeaten wife to uncover an accident-victim scam.

Written by Stephen Miller; directed by Harry Harris.

Guest stars included Kenneth McMillan, James Ward, John Zee, and Yvonne Perry.

Ken McMillan played Valerie Harper's boss on Rhoda.

Episode 8.4—*Tigers Fan* (11/11/87)

Magnum's police friend Lieutenant Tanaka is killed, and his investigation leads to a cover-up, switched identities, and drugs.

Written by Bruce Cervi; directed by Harry Harris.

Guest stars included Kwan Hi Lim, Nobu McCarthy, David Ige, James Karen, and Carlos Romero.

Episode 8.5—*Forever in Time* (11/11/87)

While helping Higgins with an historical project, Magnum becomes enamored with a beautiful married woman. Later, he receives a photograph of himself with the same woman—a Hawaiian Princess who died in 1910.

Written by Kimmer Ringwald; directed by Jackie Cooper.

Guest stars included Lelmaa Richmond, Gregg Henry, Gillian Dobb, and Elisha Cook.

Director Jackie Cooper, a former child actor, worked with me on Baa Baa Black Sheep *and was very supportive. I was the least experienced actor on that show and was more concerned with combing my hair than acting. Cooper showed me the ropes back then. He also had a pet name for me: Hugh Hefner.*

Episode 8.6—*The Love that Lies* (11/18/87)

Magnum helps his friend, Carol, with a secret about her private life and her true birthright.

Written by Jeri Taylor; directed by Ray Danton.

Guest stars included Kathleen Lloyd, Celeste Holm, and Eileen Brennan.

I played a decoy—a woman dressed in drag—to throw off the bad guys. The scene had me run into an elevator where my high heel got stuck in the elevator door.

Celeste Holm was in some classic movies: All About Eve, Gentleman's Agreement *(for which she won an Academy Award),* The Snake Pit, *and* The Tender Trap.

Eileen Brennan played Goldie Hawn's commanding officer in Private Benjamin. *She won an Emmy for recreating the same role for the TV series.*

Episode 8.7—*A Girl Named Sue* (1/13/88)
In a case of sibling rivalry over the suspicious death of a wealthy man, Magnum teams up with a novice detective whom he was once locked in a vault with.

Written by Stephen A. Miller; directed by Russ Mayberry.

Guest stars included Carol Burnett, Shelley Smith, John Calvin, and George Coe.

Episode 8.8—*Unfinished Business* (1/20/88)
Magnum's archenemy, Quang Ki, released for insufficient evidence in his attempt on Magnum's life, thrusts Thomas into a quagmire of intrigue endangering a sensitive POW/MIA prisoner exchange.

Written by Chris Abbott-Fish and Jeri Taylor; directed by Russ Mayberry.

Guest stars included Richard Narita, Marta DuBois, Kristen Carreira, Lance LeGault, and Bob Harker.

Episode 8.9—*The Great Hawaiian Adventure Company* (1/27/88)
While Magnum pitches a new business venture, T. C.'s son, Bryant, gets arrested as a result of his association with an outlaw motorcycle gang.

Written by Jeri Taylor; directed by Ray Danton.

Guest stars included Shavar Ross, Shanna Reed, and Danny Nucci.

Director Ray Danton was a former movie and TV star who lived in Hawaii. He starred in The George Raft Story. *When he came to work on* Magnum, P. I., *he had cancer, but never complained about the pain he was in. He died in 1992.*

Episode 8.10—*The Legend of the Lost Art* (2/10/88)
In an episode right out of the *Indiana Jones* movies, Magnum and his friends outmaneuver villains as they try to locate a lost ancient art scroll.

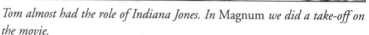

Tom almost had the role of Indiana Jones. In Magnum *we did a take-off on the movie.*

Written by Jay Huguely; directed by Burt Brinckerhoff.

Guest stars included Margaret Colin, Anthony Newley, and Kabir Bedi.

Tom wore the same Indiana Jones *outfit from the movie that he was originally supposed to star in. I was placed on a long board where knives were thrown at me, but in reality, they popped out from behind the board. Somehow, I moved my head and one of the knives popped out and cut my ear, drawing blood.*

In another scene, Tom was driving a truck, and Roger and I were on the running board when we hit a pothole and I fell off. Roger went to speak to me and saw me lying in the road laughing.

Margaret Colin played Tom's girlfriend in the movie Three Men and a Baby.

Episode 8.11—*Transitions* (2/17/88)
Robin Masters' new manuscript is stolen and an attempt on Higgins' life complicates Magnum's search.

Written by Chris Abbott-Fish; directed by Harry Harris.

Guest stars included Shavar Ross, Eugene Roche, Ray Buktenica, Phyllis Davis, and Randy Brooks.

Episode 8.12—*Resolutions* (2 hours, 5/1/88)
Unexpectedly called back to Hawaii during a family visit to Virginia, Magnum goes in search of his daughter and a former girlfriend's attacker. Meanwhile, Rick plans to marry, T. C. considers reconciling with his ex-wife, and Higgins may be Robin Masters after all.

Written by Stephen A. Miller and Chris Abbott-Fish; directed by Burt Brinckerhoff.

Guest stars included Gwen Verdon, Patrice Martinez, Jean Bruce Scott, Hal Williams, Lance LeGault, Howard Duff, Phyllis Davis, Fay Hauser, Brandon Call, Joe Regalbuto, and Kristen Carreira.

This was the final Magnum, P. I. *episode and about half of the U.S. television population saw the show. It ended in the chapel where my bride-to-be, played by Phyllis Davis, said "I do," and I got tongue-tied. At that moment, Tom said, "Goodnight, folks."*

Aloha!

Index

About the Authors

efore costarring in *Magnum, P.I.* for eight years, Larry Manetti costarred in several TV series including *Battlestar Galactica* and *Baa Baa Black Sheep*. He has also appeared in feature films, TV movies, and other television series including *Renegade, Tales from the Darkside,* and *Walker, Texas Ranger.*

Manetti is also a gourmet chef who has cooked his specialties on TV talk shows. He is the owner of Lorenzo Productions, and a former national spokesman for the Exchange Club Foundation for the Prevention of Child Abuse.

Co-author Chip Silverman is Vice President of Government Relations and Addictions Programs for Magellan Health Services Incorporated in Baltimore, Maryland. Over the past twenty years Chip has written for the *Baltimore News-American*, served as a contributing editor for *Baltimore Magazine*, and produced segments for the *Evening/PM Magazine* television show. He has appeared in the movies . . . *And Justice for All, Diner,* and *Tin Men,* and the television series *Homicide*—all courtesy of his close friend, Oscar-winning director Barry Levinson, who wrote the foreword to Chip Silverman's book, *Diner Guys.* Chip's latest, co-authored with Bob Litwin, is *The Block*, a historical mystery set in Baltimore's red-light district.

Larry met Chip when he optioned *The Block* for Lorenzo Productions.

Also available from
RENAISSANCE BOOKS

Party of Five: The Unofficial Companion
by Brenda Scott Royce
ISBN: 1-58063-000-6 • $14.95

Hercules & Xena: The Unofficial Companion
by James Van Hise
ISBN: 1-58063-001-4 • $15.95

Alien Nation: The Unofficial Companion
by Ed Gross
ISBN: 1-58063-002-2 • $14.95

Law & Order: The Unofficial Companion
by Kevin Courrier and Susan Green
ISBN: 1-58063-022-7 • $16.95

The Girl's Got Bite: An Unofficial Guide to Buffy's World
by Kathleen Tracy
ISBN: 1-58063-035-9 • $14.95

The Dukes of Hazzard: The Unofficial Companion
by David Hofstede
ISBN: 1-58063-038-3 • $14.95

Homicide: Life on the Street: The Unofficial Companion
by David P. Kalat
ISBN: 1-58063-021-9 • $16.95

Hogan's Heroes: Behind the Scenes at Stalag 13
by Brenda Scott Royce
ISBN: 1-58063-031-6 • $14.95

That Lawyer Girl: The Unauthorized Guide to Ally's World
by A. C. Beck
ISBN: 1-58063-044-8 • $14.95

To order please call
1-800-452-5589